Louisa County, Virginia
Deed Book Abstracts
1742-1744

Ruth and Sam Sparacio

The Antient Press Collection
from

Colonial Roots
Harbeson, Delaware
2017

ISBN 978-1-68034-398-4

Originally printed 2002 by The Antient Press
Printed in the United States of America

Louisa County Deed Book A
1742 - 1754

p. 1 <u>Louisa County Deed Book A 13th December 1742</u>

-This Indenture made the first day of December or in the Sixteenth year of the Reign of our Sovereign Lord George the second by the Grace of God of Great Brittain France and Ireland King Defender of the Faith &c. and in the year of our Lord one thousand seven hundred and forty two. Between JOHN SNELSON of the parish of Saint Paul and County of Hanover Gent. of the one part and JAMES POWER of the parish of Saint John and the County of King William Gent. of the other part. Witnesseth that the said JOHN SNELSON for and in consideration of the sum of five shillings to him in hand paid by the said JAMES POWER at or before the ensealing and delivery of these presents the receipt whereof he the said JOHN doth hereby acknowledge hath bargained and sold and by these presents doth bargain and sell unto the said JAMES POWER one certain tract or parcel of Land situate, lying and being in the Parish of Fredericksville & County of Louisa containing by estimation six hundred & forty seven acres be the same more or less being part of the land that was granted to CRISTOPHER SMITH late of Hanover County deceased by letters patent & by him Devised to the said JOHN SNELSON by Will fully proved & Recorded in the County Court of Hanover & bounded as follows Beginning at ALEXANDER FREEMAN's Corner stake near a small pine running North sixty five West two hundred poles to his corner Water Oak and Slash in SYMS line thence along the same North thirty four east ninety six poles to two red oak and a Hickory saplin in a Slash thence along another of his lines North ten Degrees East one hundred & sixty four poles to his & Maj. MORRIS' corner white oak thence along MORRIS' line South 70 Degrees east one hundred forty nine poles to a red oak and Hickory Bushes in a bottom thence along the Dividing line between the said POWER and Mr. JOHN SNELSON South twenty three degrees East four hundred fifty two poles to a corner pine in ROBERT ESTES line in the head of CHRISTOPHER's Run thence along his line South Eighty Degrees West two hundred and fourteen poles to the corner pine in a Slash thence North sixty Degrees West twenty poles to a pine in ALEXANDER FREEMAN's line thence along the same North thirty three Degrees and a half East One hundred and eighty

p. 2 <u>Louisa County Deed Book A 13th December 1742</u>

Four poles to the place where it first began. Together with all the woods, underwoods, trees, ways, waters, watercourses, profits, commodities, hereditaments and appurtenances to the said premises belonging or in any wise appertaining and the reversion and reversions remainder and remainders rents issues and profits thereof and of every part and parcel thereof To Have and To Hold all and singular the premises herein before mentioned or intended to be hereby bargained and sold with their and every of their appurtenances unto the said JAMES POWER his Executors Administrators and assigns from the day next before the day of the date hereof for and during and unto the full end of tenor of one whole year from thence next ensuing fully be compleated and ended Yielding and paying therefore the rent of one Ear of Indian Corn upon the last day of the said tenor, if the same shall be law fully demanded to the intent & purpose that by virtue of presents and of the stature for transferring use unto possession he the said JAMES POWER may be in the more full & actual possession of the said premises and there the better enabled to accept and take or grant & return of the Reversion and Inheritance thereof to him and his heirs. In Witness whereof the said JOHN SNELSON has to these presents set his hand & seal the day and year first above written. Sealed & Delivered in the presence of

CH. BARRET, BARTTELOT ANDERSON JOHN SNELSON
ROBERT ESTES, JOHN CARR

At a Court held for Louisa County on Monday the XIII day of December 1742. This Indenture was proven by the oaths of CH. BARRET, BARTTELOT ANDERSON & JOHN CARR three of the Witnesses thereto and Ordered to be recorded.

Test JA. LITTLEPAGE, Clk
Truly Recorded by JA. LITTLEPAGE, Clk.

p. Louisa County Deed Book A 13th December 1742

3 -This Indenture made the second day of December in the sixteenth year of the Reign of our Sovereign Lord George the second by the Grace of God of Great Britain France and Ireland King Defender of the Faith &c. and in the year of our Lord one thousand seven hundred and forty two. Between JOHN SNELSON of the Parish of Saint Paul and County of Hanover Gent. of the one part and JAMES POWER of Saint John and County of King William Gent. of the other part. Witnesseth that the said JOHN SNELSON for the love and Friendship that he bears to the said JAMES POWER and for the sum of five shillings to him in hand paid by the said JAMES POWER at or before the ensealing and delivery of these presents the receipt whereof he doth hereby acknowledge Hath granted bargained sold aliened Released and Confirmed and by these presents doth grant bargain sell alien release and confirm unto the said JAMES POWER in his full and actual possession now being by force and virtue of one Indenture of demise Bargain and sale to him thereof made for one whole year by Indenture bearing date the day next before the day of the date of these and by force of the Statute for Transferring uses into possession and to his heirs and assigns for ever one certain tract or parcel of land situate, lying and being in the parish of Fredericksville and County of Louisa containing by estimation six hundred and forty seven acres [be the same more or less] being part of the land that was granted to CHRISTOPHER SMITH late of Hanover County deceased by Letters patent and by him devised to the said JOHN SNELSON and bounded as followeth, beginning at ALEXANDER FREEMAN's Corner stake near a small pine running North sixty five West two

p. Louisa County Deed Book A 13th December 1742

4 hundred poles to his corner Water Oak and Slash in SYMS line thence along the same North thirty four east ninety six poles to two red oak and a Hickory saplin in a Slash thence along another of his lines North ten Degrees East one hundred & sixty four poles to his & Maj. MORRIS' corner white oak thence along MORRIS' line South seventy Degrees east one hundred forty nine poles to a red oak and Hickory Bushes in a bottom

thence along the Dividing line between the said POWER and Mr. JOHN SNELSON South twenty three degrees East four hundred fifty two poles to a corner pine in ROBERT ESTES line in the head of CHRISTOPHER's Run thence along his line South Eighty Degrees West two hundred and fourteen poles to the corner pine in a Slash thence North sixty Degrees West twenty poles to a pine in ALEXANDER FREEMAN's line thence along the same North thirty three Degrees and a half East One hundred and eighty Four poles to the place where it first began. Together with all the woods, underwoods, trees, ways, waters, watercourses, profits, commodities, hereditaments and appurtenances to the said premises belonging or in any wise appertaining and the reversion and reversions remainder and remainders rents issues and profits thereof and of every part and parcel thereof To Have and To Hold all and singular the premises herein before mentioned or intended to be hereby bargained and sold with their and every of their appurtenances unto the said JAMES POWER his heirs assigns to the only proper use and behoof of him the said JAMES POWER his heirs and assigns for ever and the said JOHN SNELSON for himself his heirs Executors and Administrators doth covenant promise and grant and with the said JAMES POWER his heirs and assigns by these presents that he the said JOHN SNELSON now and at the time of the sealing and delivery of these presents is lawfully and absolutely seised of and in singular the premises hereby granted and released of a good sure perfect and indefeasible Estate of Inheritance in Fee simple and hath

p. <u>Louisa County Deed Book A 13th December 1742</u>

5 in himself good right true title and lawful and absolute authority to grant and release the same in manner and form aforesaid And that he the said JAMES POWER his heirs and assigns shall and may from time to time and at all times hereafter peaceably and quietly have hold use and occupy possess and enjoy the said premises without the let suit trouble molestation interruption or hindrance of him the said JOHN SNELSON or any other person or persons whatsoever. In Witness whereof the said JOHN SNELSON hath to these presents set his hand and seal the day and year first above written.

Sealed and Delivered in presence of

CHS. BARRET, BARTTELOT ANDERSON JOHN SNELSON [seal]
ROBERT ESTES, JOHN CARR

Received of JAMES POWER five shillings current money being the consideration money within mentioned this 2nd day of December 1742.

CHS. BARRET, BARTTELOT ANDERSON JOHN SNELSON
JOHN CARR, ROBERT ESTES

At a Court held for Louisa County on Monday the XIII day of December 1742.
This Indenture and Receipt were proved by the Oaths of CHARLES BARRET, BARTTELOT ANDERSON and JOHN CARR three of the Witnesses thereto and Ordered to be recorded.

Test JAMES LITTLEPAGE, Clk.
Truly Recorded by JAS. LITTLEPAGE, Clk.

p. <u>Louisa County Deed Book A 13th December 1742</u>

6 -Know all men by these presents that we JOSEPH BUCKLEY, JOHN CARR and JOHN POINDEXTER of the parish of [blank] in the County of Louisa are held and firmly bound unto our Sovereign Lord the King his heirs and successors in the sum of One thousand pounds sterling to which payment will and truly to be made we bind our selves and every of us our and every our heirs Exors. and Admrs. jointly and severally firmly by these presents sealed with our seals and dated this Thirteenth day of December in the XVI year of the Reign of our said Lord the King Anno q Dom 1742. The condition of this Obligation is such that whereas the above bound JOSEPH BUCKLEY hath obtained a Commission from the Honble. the Lt. Governor appointing him Sherif of the County of Louisa &c. therefore the said JOSEPH BUCKLEY shall well and truly collect and duly pay his Majesty's Quitrents and all Fines and Amerciaments assessed within in the said County and also collect all Officers Fees put into his hands and duly pay the same to the respective Creditors to whom the same shall belong or such other person or persons as shall be authorized and impowered to receive the same and in all things well and truly perform the Office of Sherif then this Obligation to be void Otherwise to be and remain in full force and virtue.

JO. BUCKLEY [seal] JOHN CARR [seal] JOHN POINDEXTER [seal]

At a Court held for Louisa County on Monday the XIII day of December 1742.
This Bond acknowledged by the subscribers thereto and ordered to be recorded.

Test JAMES LITTLEPAGE, Clk.
Truly recorded by JAS. LITTLEPAGE, Clk.

p. <u>Louisa County Deed Book A 13th December 1742</u>

7 -This Indenture made the Eighth day of January in the year of our Lord one thousand seven hundred forty two Between CHARLES MOORMAN of the parish of Saint Martins in the County of Louisa planter of the one part and JAMES BUCHANNAN of the same parish and county of the other part. The said CHARLES MOORMAN in consideration of Twenty pounds current money to him in hand paid by the said JAMES BUCHANNAN before sealing and delivery of these presents the receipt whereof the said CHARLES MOORMAN doth herby acknowledge hath granted bargained sold aliened enfeoffed and confirmed by these presents doth grant, bargain sell alien enfeoff and confirm unto the said JAMES BUCHANNAN his heirs and assigns four hundred and three acres of land lying and being in the County of Louisa or both sides of Rockey Creek and Bounded as followeth, to wit, Beginning at PRICES corner and along his line South sixty three Degrees East at seven poles Rockey Creek in all seventy nine poles to a pine in the [unreadable] line thence south thirty nine degrees thirty minutes west one hundred and twenty poles to a red oak land two white oaks saplins thence south sixty three Degrees west at the said Crick Eighteen poles in all two hundred and ninety poles to a white oak on the side of a branch thence North sixty three degrees west two hundred and forty three poles to corner several oak saplins thence North sixty eight Degrees East five hundred and thirty poles to a pine in the said PRICEs land and or along the same South Three Degrees East fifty two poles to the Beginning this being the bounds of the Patent and being in all four hundred Eighty three acres of which I do except

Eighty acres of land at the lower end of the tract it being a part of the same Dividend lying and being on both sides of Rockey Creek from the line of ALEXANDER GALASPA to him or his heirs or assigns and the remainder part of the tract of land being four hundred and three acres being the upper end of the tract lying on both sides of Rockey Creek I do bargaine sell make over to JAMES BUCHANNAN to him or his heirs Executors Administrators or assigns and all woods, ways waters profits and emoluments whatsoever belonging to the said four hundred and three acres of land lying on both sides of Rockey Creek belonging or appertaining and the reversions remainder and remainders thereof and every part and parcel thereof and all the right title and interest whatsoever of him the said CHARLES MOORMAN in and to the said

p. <u>Louisa County Deed Book A 10th January 1742</u>

8 bargained premises and appurtenances and every part and parcel thereof To Have and to hold the said tract of land and all and singular the premises with the appurtenances unto the said JAMES BUCHANNAN his heirs and assigns forever to the only proper use and behoof of him the said JAMES BUCHANNAN his heirs and assigns forever and the said CHARLES MOORMAN for himself his heirs executors and administrators doth by these presents covenant promise and agree to and with the said JAMES BUCHANNAN that he the said CHARLES MOORMAN at the time of sealing and delivery of these presents fixed his hands seized of and indefeasable state of Inheritance in Fee Simple in the said land premises and hath clear absolute lawful Right and authority to sell and convey the same in Manner and form aforesaid JAMES BUCHANNAN his heirs and assigns shall and may forever hereinafter peaceably and quietly Have hold possess and enjoy all and singular the premises and appurtenances having or law fully claiming only Estate right or title in or to the same or any part of and the said CHARLES MOORMAN and his heirs shall and forever defend by these presents the aforesaid tract of land and premises with the appurtenances unto the said JAMES BUCHANNAN his heirs and assigns against him the said CHARLES MOORMAN and his heirs and all or any other person or persons having or law fully claiming any such right or title to the same or any part or parcel hereafter in Witness whereof the said parties have hereunto interchangeably set their hands and affixed their seals the day and year above written. Sealed and Delivered in presence of

JOHN SMITHSON, SALIM BOCOCK CHARLES X [his mark] MOORMAN [seal]

Received of JAMES BUCHANNAN twenty pounds current money the full consideration within mentioned January 1742. Witness JOHN SMITHSON SALIM BOCOCK

CHARLES X [his mark] MOORMAN [seal]

Memorandum that on this Eighth Day of January DCCXXXXII Livery of Seisen of the within mentioned premises with the appurtenances made by CHARLES MOORMAN of the said JAMES BUCHANNAN his heirs and assigns forever according to the form and effect of the within Indenture. In presence of JOHN SNELSON, SAL. BOCOCK

At a Court held for Louisa County on Monday 10th day of January 1742.

This Indenture Receipt and Memorandum of Livery and Seisen were acknowledged by CHARLES MOORMAN

p. Louisa County Deed Book A 10th January 1742

9 one of the parties and Ordered to be Recorded.

Test JAMES LITTLEPAGE, Clk.
Truly recorded by LITTLEPAGE, Clerk

-This Indenture made this Eighth Day of January in the year of our Lord one Thousand seven hundred forty two. Between CHARLES MOORMAN of the parish of Saint Martins in the County of Louisa planter of the one part and ALEXANDER GALASPA of the same County of the other part. Witnesseth that the said CHARLES MOORMAN for the consideration on hand paid by the said ALEXANDER GALASPA before sealing and delivery of these presents the receipt whereof the said CHARLES MOORMAN doth hereby acknowledge have granted bargained sold aliened enfeoffed and confirmed and by these presents doth grant bargain and sell alien enfeoff and confirm unto the said ALEXANDER GALASPA his heirs and assigns Eighty acres of land part of four hundred and eighty three acres lying and being at the lower end of the said Tract in the County of Louisa I do bargain sell make over confirm to the said GALASPA to him or his heirs executors administrators or assigns and all woods ways waters profits emoluments whatsoever belonging to the said eighty acres of land lying and being on both sides of Rockey Creek joyning to BUCHANNANS and Tract of land belonging or appertaining and the reversions remainder and remainders thereof and every part and parcel thereof and all the right title and Interest whatsoever of him the said CHARLES MOORMAN in and to the said bargained premises and appurtenances and every part and parcel thereof To have and To hold the said Tract of land and all and singular the premises with the appurtenances unto the said ALEXANDER GALASPA his heirs and assigns forever and the said CHARLES MOORMAN for him self his heirs executors administrators doth by these presents covenant and agree to and with the said ALEXANDER GALASPA that he the said CHARLES MOORMAN at the time of sealing and delivery of these presents in and hands seised of and Indefeasable estate of Inheritance in Fee Simple in the said land and premises and hath clear absolute lawfull right and authority to sell and convey the same in manner and form aforesaid ALEXANDER GALASPA his heirs and assigns such and may forever hereafter peaceably and quietly have hold possess and enjoy all and singular the premises and appurtenances with out such molestation of any person or persons whatsoever having or law fully claiming any estate right title on or to the same or any part thereof and the said CHARLES MOORMAN and his heirs shall and will warrant and forever defend by these presents the aforesaid

p. Louisa County Deed Book A 10th January 1742

10 tract of land and premises with the appurtenances unto the said ALEXANDER GALASPA his heirs and assigns against him the said CHARLES MOORMAN and his heirs and all or any other person or persons having or law fully claiming any estate right or title to the same or any part or parcel thereof in Witness whereof the said parties have hereunto interchangeably set their hands and affixed their seals the day and year above

written. Sealed and Delivered
in presence of CHARLES X [his mark] MOORMAN [seal]
JOHN SMITHSON, SALIM BOCOCK

Received of ALEXANDER GALASPA the full consideration within mentioned January 1742.
JOHN SMITHSON, SALIM BOCOCK CHARLES M. MOORMAN

Memorandum that on this Eighth Day of January MDCCXXXXII Livery of Seisen of the within mentioned premises with appurtenances made by me CHARLES MOORMAN unto the said ALEXANDER GALASPA his heirs and assigns.

for presence of
JOHN SMITHSON, SALIM BOCOCK CHARLES X [his mark] MOORMAN [seal]

At a Court held for Louisa County on Monday 10th of January 1742.
This Indenture Receipt and memorandum of Livery and Seisen were acknowledged by CHARLES MOORMAN one of the parties and Ordered to be Recorded.
Test JAMES LITTLEPAGE, Clk.
Truly recorded by LITTLEPAGE, Clerk

p. <u>Louisa County Deed Book A 10th January 1742</u>
11 -This Indenture made the Tenth day of January in the sixteenth year of the Reign of our Sovereign Lord George the second by the Grace of God of Great Brittan France and Ireland King Defender of the Faith &c. and in the year of our Lord Christ one thousand seven hundred and forty two. Between JOHN DASHPER of the parish of Fredrickville ánd County of Louisa planter of the one part and WILLIAM HENDERSON of the county of Goochland planter of the other part. Witnesseth that the said JOHN DASHPER for and in consideration of the sum of Twenty pounds current money of Virginia to him in hand paid on Interest to be paid by the said WILLIAM HENDERSON at and before the ensealing and delivery of these presents the receipt whereof he the said JOHN DASHPER doth hereby acknowledge and thereof and every part thereof doth clearly acquit and discharge the said WILLIAM HENDERSON his heirs executors administrators for ever by these presents hath given granted bargained aliened enfeoffed and confirmed and by these presents doth fully and absolutely give grant bargain sell alien enfeoff and confirm unto the said WILLIAM HENDERSON and his Heirs all their Dividend Tract of parcel of land situate lying on besides of Bever Creek in Fredericksville parish and County of Louisa containing by estimation two hundred acres be the same more or less and bounded this Viz. Beginning at several marked trees on the south side of Bever Creek on the east side or small branch runing thence North thirty degrees west two hundred and three poles to several marked trees thence North sixty one and a half degrees east two hundred & twenty two poles crossing Bever Creek to the first station together with all woods underwoods ways waters and water courses Feeding pastures easements hereditaments and appurtenances and the reversion and reversions & remainder and remainders and all and singular the estate right title property claim and demand of him the said JOHN DASHPER of in or to the premises or any part thereof with the appurtenances To Have and To Hold

p. Louisa County Deed Book A 10th January 1742

12 the said Dividend Tract or parcel of land and all and singular other the premises hereby granted bargained and sold with their and every of their appurtenances unto the said WILLIAM HENDERSON his heirs and assigns to the only proper use and behoof of the said WILLIAM HENDERSON his heirs and assigns forever and the said JOHN DASHPER for himself his heirs and said tract of parcel of land and premises with the appurtenances unto the said WILLIAM HENDERSON and his heirs against him the said JOHN DASHPER his heirs and assigns and all and every other person or person whatsoever lawfully claiming or to claim by from or under him them or any other person or person whatsoever shall and will warrant and forever defend by these presents. Witness whereof he the said JOHN DASHPER hath hereunto set his hand and seal the date above mentioned.

Sealed & Delivered JOHN DASHPER [seal]
in presence of [blank]

Memo. that Livery and Seisen of the lands and appurtenances within mentioned was given to the within named WILLIAM HENDERSON by the within named JOHN DASHPER this tenth day January one thousand and seven hundred and forty two.

Sealed and Delivered in presence of [blank] JOHN DASHPER [seal]

Received this tenth day of January one thousand seven hundred forty two of WILLIAM HENDERSON twenty pounds current money of Virginia being in full for the lands and appurtenances within mentioned I say received by me. JOHN DASHPER

At a Court held for Louisa County on Monday 10th day January 1742 This Indenture receipt and memorandum of Livery and Seisen were acknowledged by JOHN DASHPER one of the parties and ordered to be recorded. Test LITTLEPAGE, Clerk

Truly recorded by LITTLEPAGE, Clk.

p. Louisa County Deed Book A 10th January 1742

13 -This Indenture made the tenth day of January in the sixteenth year of the Reign of our Sovereign Lord George the second by the Grace of God of Great Brittain France and Ireland King Defender of the Faith &c. and in the year of our Lord Christ one thousand seven hundred and fourty two Between LAURENCE REDMAN of the Parish of Fredericksville and County of Louisa planter of the one part and WILLIAM ADAMS of the same parish and County planter of the other part. Witnesseth that the said LAURENCE REDMAN for and in consideration for the sum of five thousand pounds of lawful sweet scented Tobacco to him in hand paid secured to be paid by the said WILLIAM ADAMS at and before the ensealing and delivery of these presents the receipt whereof he the said LAURENCE REDMAN doth hereby acknowledge and thereof and every part thereof doth fully acquit and discharge the said WILLIAM ADAMS his heirs executors and administrators for ever by these presents hath Given granted bargained sold aliened enfeoffed and confirmed and by these presents doth clearly and absolutely give grant bargain sell alien enfeoff and confirm unto the said WILLIAM ADAMS and his heirs all that Dividend Tract or parcel of Land and Plantation thereon situate lying and being on the North side the South Anna river in the parish of Fredericksville and County of Louisa containing by estimation one hundred and four acres be

the same more or less and Bounded thus Viz. Beginning at WILLIAM HARRIS's corner maple on the River runing thence down the said South Anna River as it meanders making in a strait line one hundred and fifty poles to POINTERS by a Glade North twenty four degrees west one hundred and sixty one poles to a

p. Louisa County Deed Book A 10th January 1742

14 red oak in the said WILLIAM HARRIS's line Thence on the said line south fifty degrees west one hundred and five poles to the first station Together with all woods underwoods ways waters and water courses Feedings pastures easements commodities heriditaments and appurtenances whatsoever to the same belonging or in any wise appertaining, and the reversion and reversions remainder and remainders and all and singular the estate right title property claim and demand of the said LAURENCE REDMAN of in or to the premises or any part thereof with the appurtenances To Have and To Hold the said Dividend tract or parcel of land and all and singular other the premises hereby granted bargained and sold with their and every of their appurtenances unto the said WILLIAM ADAMS his heirs and assigns to the only proper person use and behoof of him the said WILLIAM ADAMS his heirs and assigns forever And the said LAURENCE REDMAN for himself and his heirs the said Tract or parcel of land and premises with the appurtenances unto the said WILLIAM ADAMS and his heirs against him the said LAURENCE REDMAN his heirs and assigns all and every other person or persons whatsoever lawfully claiming or to claim by from or under him them or any of them or any other person or persons whatsoever shall and will warrant and forever defend by these presents. In Witness whereof he the said LAURENCE REDMAN hath hereunto set his hand and seal the date above mentioned.

Signed and Delivered
in presence of J. MOORE LARRANCE X [his mark] REDMOND [seal]

Memorandum that Livery and Seisen of the Lands and appurtenances within mentioned was given to the within named WILLIAM ADAMS by the within named LAURENCE REDMAN this tenth day of January one thousand seven hundred and forty two.

Sealed & Delivered in presence of J. MOORE LARRANCE X [his mark] REDMOND [seal]

p. Louisa County Deed Book A 10th January 1742

15 Received this tenth day of January one thousand seven hundred and forty two of WILLIAM ADAMS five thousand pounds of Lawful sweet scented Tobacco it being in full for the Lands and appurtenances within mentioned I say received by me.

Test J. MOORE LARRANCE X [his mark] REDMOND

At a Court held for Louisa County on Monday the 10th day of January 1742.

This Indenture Receipt and Memorandum of Livery and Seisen were acknowledged by LAURENCE REDMOND one of the parties, Also MARY the wife of the said LAURENCE [being first privily examined] relinquished her right and title of Dower of in and unto the Lands and appurtenances within mentioned and Ordered to be Recorded.

Test JAMES LITTLEPAGE, Clk.
Truly recorded by LITTLEPAGE, Clk.

-This Indenture made the fourteenth day of February in the sixteenth year of the Reign of our Sovereign Lord George the second by the Grace of God of Great Britain France and Ireland King Defender of the Faith &c. and in the year of our Lord Christ one thousand seven hundred and fourty two Between LAURENCE REDMAN of the parish of Fredericksville and County of Louisa planter of the one part and JOHN FOSTER of the same parish and County planter of the other part Witnesseth that the said LAURENCE REDMAN for and in consideration of the sum of Two thousand five hundred pounds of Lawful sweet scented Tobacco to him in hand paid or secured to be paid by the said JOHN FOSTER at and before the ensealing and delivery of these presents the receipt whereof he the said LAURENCE REDMAN doth hereby acknowledge and thereof and every part thereof

p. Louisa County Deed Book A 14th February1742

16 clearly acquit and discharge the said JOHN FOSTER his heirs executors and administrators for ever by these presents Hath given granted bargained sold aliened Enfeoffed and confirmed and by these presents doth fully and absolutely give grant bargain sell alien enfeoff and confirm unto the said JOHN FOSTER and his heirs all the Dividend Tract or parcel of Land situate lying and being on both sides of Cubb Creek in the parish of Frederisksville and County of Louisa containing by estimation one hundred and four acres be the same more or less and bounded thus Viz. Beginning at POINTERS in WILLIAM HARRISS's line runing thence on the said line North fifty degrees East one hundred and sixty five poles crossing Cubb Creek to the back line thence south fourty two degrees East ninety poles to a pine thence south thirty eight degrees West one hundred and eighty eighty crossing the said Creek to POINTERS Thence South fourty four and half degrees East fifty poles to POINTERS Thence south fifty five degrees West twenty four poles to the first station Together with all Woods underwoods Ways Waters and Watercourses feedings pastures easements commodities hereditaments and appurtenances whatsoever to the same belonging or in any wise appertaining and the reversion and reversions Remainder and Remainders and all and singular the estate right title property claim and demand of him the said LAURENCE REDMAN in or to the premises or any part thereof with the appurtenances To Have and To Hold the said Dividend Tract or parcel of Land and all and singular other the premises hereby granted bargained and sold with their and every of their appurtenances unto the said JOHN FOSTER his heirs and assigns to the only proper use and behoof of him the said JOHN FOSTER his heirs and assigns forever. And the said LAURENCE REDMAN for himself and his heirs the said tract or parcel of land and premises with the appurtenances to the said JOHN FOSTER and his heirs against him the said LAURENCE REDMAN his heirs and assigns and all and every other person or persons whatsoever lawfully claiming or to claim by from or under him them or any of them or any other person or persons whatsoever shall and will warrant and for ever defend by these presents In Witness whereof he the said LAURENCE

p. Louisa County Deed Book A 14th February 1742

17 REDMAN hath hereunto set his hand and seal the date above mentioned.

Sealed and delivered
in presence of LAURANCE X [his mark] REDMAN [SEAL]
BALLARD SMITH, JAMES GOODALL,
JOHN X [his mark] ADAMS, WILLIAM NORVELL

Memorandum that Livery and Seisen of the Lands and appurtenances within mentioned was given to the within named JOHN FOSTER by the within named LAURENCE REDMAN this fourteenth day of February one thousand seven hundred and fourty two.

Sealed and Delivered
in presence of LAURANCE X [his makr] REDMAN [seal]
BALLARD SMITH, JAMES GOODALL
JOHN X [his mark] ADAMS, WILLIAM NORVALL

Received this fourteenth day of February one thousand seven hundred and fourty two of JOHN FOSTER the sum of two thousand five hundred pounds of lawful scented Tobacco it being in full for the Lands and Appurtenances the within mentioned I say received by me.

Test LAURANCE X [his makr] REDMAN [seal]
BALLARD SMITH, JAMES GOODALL
JOHN X [his mark] ADAMS, WILLIAM NORVALL

At a Court held for Louisa County on Monday the 14th day of February 1742.
This Indenture and Memorandum of Livery and Seisen was proved

p. <u>Louisa County Deed Book A 14th February 1742</u>
18 by the oaths of THOMAS BALLARD SMITH, JAMES GOODALL and JOHN ADAMS three of the Witnesses thereto Also MARY the wife of the said LAURENCE [being first privily examined] relinquished all her right and Title of Dower of in and unto the said Lands & appurtenances therein mentioned and Ordered to be Recorded.

Test JAMES LITTLEPAGE, Clk.
Truly Recorded by LITTLEPAGE, Clk.

-This Indenture made the Thirteenth day of February in the year of our Lord one thousand seven hundred and forty two Between JOHN KEMBREW of the County of Louisa of the one part and WILLIAM SPILLER of the County of King William of the other part Witnesseth that the said JOHN KEMBREW for and in consideration of the sum of five shillings current money to him in hand paid by the said WILLIAM at or before the ensealing and delivery of these presents the receipt whereof he doth hereby acknowledge Hath Bargained and Sold and by these presents Doth Bargain and sell unto the said WILLIAM SPILLER his Executors Administrators and assigns one certain tract or parcel of land situate lying and being in the parish of Fredericksville in the County of Louisa containing Eight hundred acres and is Bounded as follows Beginning at Mr. CHISWELLS' Corner white oak running thence along his line south thirty four Degrees West One hundred and seventy four poles to his and Col. MERIWETHER's Line South Eighty two degrees West Three hundred and four poles to a Scrubby white oak and pine saplins near a Meadow thence North twenty two degrees West two hundred and sixty poles to several red oak a white oak and pine saplins thence North sixty five degrees East two hundred and sixty poles to two pines by the side of a hill thence North Eighty six degrees East two hundred poles to two pines and a red oake bush in CHISWELL's line thence along the same south five degrees East one hundred eighty four to the beginning, which said Tract of Land was taken up by the said JOHN KEMBREW and by him patented the second day of June in the year of our Lord one thousand seven hundred and forty To Have and to Hold the said Tract or parcel of Land before mentioned or intended to be hereby

p. <u>Louisa County Deed Book A 14th February 1742</u>
19 Bargain'd and sold with their and every of their Rights Members & appurtenances unto the said WILLIAM SPILLER his Executors Administrators and assigns from the day next before the day of the date of these presents unto the full end and term of one whole year from thence next ensuing and fully to be compleated and ended Yielding and paying thereof to the said JOHN KEMBREW his heirs or assigns the Rent of one pepper corn upon the Feast day of Saint Michael the Arch Angel now next coming [if lawfully demanded] and no more To the intent and purpose that by virtue of these presents And of the Statute for Transferring uses unto said tract or parcel of land and other the premises with the appurtenances and be thereby enabled to accept and take a grant & release of the Reversion and Inheritance thereof [according to the Tenour of the Patents for the same] to him his heirs and assigns forever by Indenture intended to be made between the said JOHN KEMBREW of the one part and the said WILLIAM SPILLER of the other part and bearing date the day next after the day of the date of these presents. In Witness whereof the part to these presents have interchangeably set their hands and seals the day and year first above written. Seal'd and delivered in presence of JOHN KEMBREW [seal]
GEORGE X BERRY's mark
WM. KEMBROW, TOMMAS WASH, junior

At a Court held for Louisa County on Monday the 14th of February 1742.
This Indenture acknowledged by JOHN KEMBREW one of the parties and Ordered to be Recorded. Test JAMES LITTLEPAGE, Clk.
Truly recorded by LITTLEPAGE, Clk.

This Indenture made the Fourteenth day of February in the year of our Lord One thousand seven hundred and forty two Between JOHN KEMBREW of the County of Louisa and ELIZABETH his wife of the one part and WILLIAM SPILLER of the County of King William of the other part Witnesseth that the said JOHN KEMBREW and ELIZABETH his wife for and in consideration of the sum of twenty five pounds current money of Virginia to them in hand well and truly paid by the said WILLIAM SPILLER at and before the ensealing and delivery of these presents the Receipt whereof the said JOHN KEMBREW & ELIZABETH his wife do hereby acknowledge and thereof and of and from every part and parcel thereof do acquit release and discharge the said WILLIAM SPILLER his heirs and assigns by these presents they the said JOHN KEMBREW and ELIZABETH his wife hath granted bargained sold released and confirmed and by these presents do grant bargain sell release and confirm unto the said WILLIAM SPILLER [on his act of possession now being by virtue of a Bargain and Sale to him thereof made of the said JOHN KEMBREW by Indenture bearing date the day next before the day and date of these presents for the term of one year commencing from the day before the day of the date of the said Indenture and by force of the Statute for transferring used into possession and to his heirs for ever two Patents for Eight hundred acres of Land situate lying and being in the parish of Fredericksville in the said County of Louisa and is Bounded as followeth Beginning at Mr. CHISWELLS' Corner white oak running thence along his line south thirty four Degrees West One hundred and seventy four poles to his and Col. MERIWETHER's Line South Eighty two degrees West Three hundred and four poles to a Scrubby white oak and pine saplins near a Meadow thence North twenty two degrees West two hundred and sixty poles to several red oaks a white oak and pine saplins thence North sixty five degrees East two hundred and sixty poles to two pines by the side of

p. Louisa County Deed Book A 14th February 1742

21 a hill thence North Eighty six degrees East two hundred poles to two pines and a red oake bush in CHISWELL's line thence along the same south five degrees East one hundred eighty four to the beginning, which said Tract of Land was taken up by the said JOHN KEMBREW and by him patented the second day of June in the year of our Lord one thousand seven hundred and forty. And all the estate right title use trust possession property profit claim Interest and Demand whatsoever of them the said JOHN and ELIZABETH his wife in or to the same or any Tract or parcel thereof To Have and To hold the said tract or parcel of Land herein before mentioned and all and singular other the premises intended to be hereby granted or released with their and every of their rights members and appurtenances unto the said WILLIAM SPILLER his heirs and assigns to the use and behoof of the said WILLIAM SPILLER his heirs and assigns forever provided he will cultivate and improve the same according as the Law directs. And the said JOHN and ELIZABETH his wife their heirs executors and administrators the said is hereby granted and released premises and every part and parcel thereof with their appurtenances unto the said WILLIAM SPILLER his heirs and assigns against the said JOHN and ELIZABETH his wife their heirs and assigns shall and will warrant and forever defend by these presents. And that they the said JOHN and ELIZABETH his wife now have in themselves good right full power and lawful and absolute authority to grant bargain sell release and confirm the said piece or parcel of land and other the premises above mentioned or intended to be hereby granted and released with their and every of their appurtenances unto the said WILLIAM SPILLER his heirs and assigns forever in manner and form aforesaid. And that free and clear and freely and clearly acquitted exonerated discharged or otherwise will and sufficiently defended kept harmless and indemnified by the said JOHN and ELIZABETH his wife their heirs executors and administrators of from and against all and all manner of former and other gifts grants bargains sales leases Jointures Dowers and Titles of Dower uses Wills, Intents, Mortgages Executors Fines Americaments Quitrents and all arrearages thereof and of and from all other estates or titles whatsoever In Witness whereof the parties to these

p. Louisa County Deed Book A 14th February 1742
22 presents have interchangeably set their hands and seals the day and year first above written. Signed Seal'd & deliver'd
in presence of JOHN KEMBREW [seal]
GEORGE B. BERRY's mark ELIZABETH E [her mark] KEMBREW [seal]
WILLM. KEMBREW, TOMMAS WASH, junior

At a Court held for Louisa County on Monday the 14th day of February 1742.
This Indenture acknowledged by JOHN KEMBREW one of the parties and Ordered to be Recorded. Test JAMES LITTLEPAGE, Clk.
Truly Recorded by LITTLEPAGE, Clk.

Dedimus for Exam of KEMBREW } George the second by the Grace of God of Great Britain France Ireland King Defender of the Faith &c. To CHARLES BARRET, JOHN CARR and JOHN POINDEXTER Gent. Justices of Louisa County Greeting: Whereas JOHN KEMBREW of the said County of Louisa and ELIZABETH his wife have conveyed to WILLIAM SPILLER of King George County the fee simple estate of in and unto a certain Tract or parcel of land containing eight hundred acres being in the said County of Louisa and parish of Fredericksville with the appurtenances as by a certain Indenture of Release bearing date the XIV day of February MDCCXLII hereto annexed appears And whereas we are informed that the said ELIZABETH is so sickly and impotent that she is unable to travel to the Court of our said County of Louisa to make such acknowledgment of her Dower as in that case is required. Therefore we the state of the said ELIZABETH comisserating have given you or any two of you power to take the acknowledgment of the said ELIZABETH shall be willing to make concerning the premises

p. Louisa County Deed Book A 14th February 1742
23 Hereby Commanding that you or two of you do personally go to the said ELIZABETH and her privily and a part from her said Husband to examine touching her consent and receive her acknowledgment aforesaid and that you certifie the same and make your return thereof under your seals to our Justices at the Court house of our said County of Louisa that the same together with the Deed aforesaid may be recorded sending therewith to the same Justices this Writ Witness JAMES LITTLEPAGE Clerk of our said County Court of Louisa the XIV day of March in the XVI year of our Reign Anno q Dom 1742, JAMES LITTLEPAGE

In Compliance with the above order we the subscribers met this day at the house of JOHN KEMBREW and examined his wife ELIZABETH KEMBREW privily and apart from her husband who freely relinquishes her right of Dower to the eight hundred acres of land in the Deed to M. SPILLER hereto annexed witness our hands and seals this 26 April 1743.
CHARLES BARRET [seal] JOHN CARR [seal]

-This Indenture Tripartile made the twelfth day of August in the year of our Lord one thousand seven hundred and forty two Between PATRICK BARCLAY of the County of King and QUEEN MERCHANT of the first part and JOHN MARTAIN of the second part And

ELIZABETH MARTIN Spinster daughter of the said JOHN of the third part Whereas there is a Marriage intended by the Grace of God shortly to be had and solemnized between the said PATRICK BARCLAY and ELIZABETH and Whereas the said JOHN MARTIN by Deed of Gift recorded in the General Court hath conveyed and settled in Fee upon the said ELIZABETH a certain parcel or tract of land in Goochland County on James River containing six hundred acres or there abouts together with [blank] slave ESTER and her increase in by the said Deed may more fully appear And whereas the said JOHN hath agreed together with the said PATRICK the sum of four hundred pounds sterling money of Great Britain as a Marriage portion with the said ELIZABETH now the Indenture Witnesseth that the said PATRICK BARCLAY for and in consideration of the said Marriage portion and for and hereunto a pension for the said ELIZABETH [provided the said Marriage the effect] hath

p. Louisa County Deed Book A 14th February 1742

24 and by these presents doth grant alien release and confirm unto the said JOHN MARTIN all that piece parcel or tract of land situate in the parish of [blank] and County of Hanover which the said PATRICK lately purchased of the Executors of WILLIAM JOHNSON deceased containing nine hundred acres or thereabouts in as full and ample manner as he the said PATRICK now enjoys in Hanover Court together with Twenty Slaves [namely BELINDA, IRIS, LYDIA, DINA, PEACH, TOM, ROBIN, JO, ENDINGBURGH, GLASCOW, ROGER, LONDON, JACK, young JO, DAVY, WILL, NED, MOLL, NANNY and ESTER] and the reversion and Remainder of the said last mentioned slaves and land and all the estate whatsoever either in Law or equity of him the said PATRICK of in or to the said last mentioned Land and Slaves and increase To Have and to hold the said last mentioned parcel or tract of land and slaves and their increase unto the said JOHN MARTIN his heirs and assigns upon the several trusts and uses hereafter declared [that is to say] to the use of the said PATRICK during the joint lives of him and the said ELIZABETH and in case the said ELIZABETH shall survive the said PATRICK then to her for her life and the issue Male of their two Bodies begotten and upon failure of issue Males then to the heir or heirs female of their two bodies begotten equally to be divided between them And for want of such heir or heirs or in case there be such heir or heirs Male or female at the time of the death of the said PATRICK and they shall all dye or that none of them Male or female shall Marry or arrive to the age of twenty one years then to the right heirs of said PATRICK after the said ELIZABETH decrease Never the less in the said ELIZABETH shall happen to survive the said PATRICK it shall be at the election either to take and accept of one third part of all such personall Estate as the said PATRICK shall have at the time of his death together with Dower in her real estate or else to stand and abide by these presents and the provision hereby made for her [provided such election be made within nine months after the deced.

p. Louisa County Deed Book A 14th February 1742

25 of the said PATRICK] any thing herein to the contrary Notes the sending and the said ELIZABETH doth by these presents [in consideration of the said four hundred pounds sterling] renounce and relinquish all Interest right & title whatsoever that she now hath or

ever had of in or to the said parcel or tract of land in Goochland County on James River aforesaid And all and every the slave and slaves aforesaid and their increase to her given by her said Father as aforesaid And the same doth surrender and give up unto the said JOHN MARTIN and his heirs and assigns forever And the said PATRICK BARCLAY and ELIZABETH MARTIN do and each of them doth for their and each of their heirs for Admors. and assigns covenant promise and agree to and with the said JOHN MARTIN his heirs Exors. Admos. and assigns that [provided the said intended Marriage take effect] they or either of them will at any time for ever hereafter all the request of the said JOHN MARTIN his heirs or assigns or of any other person in his or their behalf make do and execute any other matter cause or thing Material & in Law Necessary for the more sure and certain Conveying the confirming the said piece and Tract of Land on James River and the aforesaid slaves thereto annexed in fee simple unto the said JOHN MARTIN his heirs and assigns according to the true intent and meaning of these presents. In Witness whereof the parties to these presents have interchangeably set their hands and seals the day and year first above written.

Seal'd & deliv'd in presence of

AND. BARCLAY, MORD THROCKMORTON — PATT [seal] BARCLAY

FRANCIS JERDONE, ARCH. GORDON — JN. [seal] MARTIN

JOHN MARTIN — ELIZ. [seal] MARTIN

Received the sum of Four hundred pounds sterling being the sum mentioned I say rece'd 400 Ster. the day & year first within mentioned.

Present JOHN MARTIN, AND. BARCLAY — PATT BARCLAY

p. <u>Louisa County Deed Book A 14th February 1742</u>

26 At a Court held for Louisa County on Monday the 14th day of February 1742.

This Indenture was acknowledged by PATRICK BARCLAY one of the parties and as to the Execution thereof by JOHN MARTIN and ELIZABETH MARTIN the other parties the same was proved by the Oaths of ANDREW BARCLAY and MORDICA THROCKMORTON and FRANCIS JERDONE three of the Witnesses thereto and Ordered to be Recorded.

Test JAMES LITTLEPAGE, Clk.

Truly Recorded by LITTLEPAGE, Clk.

-This Indenture made this eighth day of December in the sixteenth year of the Reign of our Sovereign Lord George the second by the Grace of God of Great Britain France and Ireland King Defender of the Faith &c. in the year of our Lord Christ one thousand seven hundred and forty two By and Between BENJAMIN BROWN of the parish of Saint Martin in the County of Hanover of the one part and CLEAVERS DUKE of the said parish and County of the other part Witnesseth that he the said BENJAMIN BROWN for and in consideration of the sum of one hundred and twenty pound good and lawful money of Virginia to him in hand paid by the said CLEAVERS DUKE the receipt whereof he doth hereby acknowledge hath granted bargained and sold aliened released and confirmed and by these presents unto the said CLEAVERS DUKE and his heirs and assigns for ever one tract and parcel of land containing four hundred and twenty three acres be the same more or less situate lying and being in the parish of Saint Martins in the County of Louisa which said Land is bounded as followeth Viz. Beginning at a White oake on the South side of the Little River JAMES YANCEY Mill running thence south ten degrees West one hundred poles to DAVID CRENSHAW corner white oake saplin thence south eighty degrees east two hundred and sixty four poles to a white oake and Mulberry in a branch near RICHMOND TERREL's fence thence up the said Branch South twenty degrees West fifty six poles to a white oake in the said Branch then south forty one degrees East two hundred and sixteen poles to JOHN TAIT

p. Louisa County Deed Book A 14th February 1742

27 corner thirteen {unreadable] North sixty degrees East fourty six poles to a Spanish oake in BRADLEYs line thence on the said BRADLEYs line North one hundred and twenty poles and an half to RICHARD THURMANs line thence on the said THURMANs line South seventy five degrees West to a Corner white oake fifty two poles thence North seventeen degrees West one hundred and two pole to a corner thence South fifty degrees East one hundred and thirty two poles to the River thence up the same by the Water course making in a Straight line four hundred and twenty one poles to the beginning which said land was granted to the said BENJAMIN BROWN by certain patent bearing date the twenty second day of February one thousand seven hundred and twenty four which said land bounded as aforesaid together with all houses orchards gardens fences woods underwoods waters and watercourses there as standing growing and being with all profits comodities advantages and appurtenances whatsoever to the same belonging or in any wise appertaining And also the reversion and reversions Remainder and remainders thereof and of every part and parcel thereof To Have and To Hold the said Tract or parcel of land as above bounded with there and every of there appurtenances unto the said CLEAVERS DUKE and to his heirs and assigns for ever to the only use and behoof of him the said CLEAVERS DUKE his heirs and assigns that he and the said BENJAMIN BROWN for himself and his heirs doth covenant grant and agree to and with the said CLEAVERS DUKE his heirs and assigns that he and they shall and may at all times hereafter peaceably and quietly possess hold & enjoy the said Granted Land and premises free and clear from all future sales Gifts Grants Mortgages rights of Dower or any other incumbrances whatsoever And he the said BENJAMIN BROWN and his heirs shall and will warrant and forever defend the said Granted Land and premises with the appurtenances unto the said CLEAVERS DUKE his heirs and assigns forever against all other person or persons that shall lay claim thereunto And further that the said BENJAMIN BROWN and his heirs and assigns shall and will do and Execute all such further Act or Deed for the further and better of the said granted land and premises as the said CLEAVERS DUKE or his heirs

p. Louisa County Deed Book A 14th February 1742

28 and assigns or their Council in the Law shall and will deliver or acquire. In Witness whereof the said BENJAMIN BROWN hath hereunto set his hand and affixed his seal the day and year first above written.

Signed Sealed & Delivered

in the presence of us BENJA. BROWN [seal]
THOMAS LANKFORD, WILLIAM B [his mark] BOND
BENJA. DUMAS

Memorandum that on the Eighth day of November one thousand seven hundred and fourty two quiet and peaceable possession and seizen of the within granted land and premises was made done and delivered by the within named BENJAMIN BROWN to the within mentioned CLEAVERS DUKE according to the form and effect of the within written Deed.

In the presence of BENJA. BROWN [seal]
BENJA. DUMAS, THOS. LANKFORD, WM. B [his mark] BOND

At a Court held for Louisa County on Monday 14th day of February 1742.
This Indenture and Memorandum of Livery and Seisen were acknowledged by BENJAMIN BROWN one of the parties and Ordered to be Recorded.

Test JAMES LITTLEPAGE, Clk.
Truly Recorded by LITTLEPAGE, Clk.

-This Indenture made this forten day of febry in the year of our Lord Christ one thousand seven hundred and forty tow between AMBROSE JOSHUA SMITH of the parish of Fredrickville in the County of Louisa of the one part and BENJAMIN HENSON of the aforesaid parish and County of the other part

p. Louisa County Deed Book A 14th February 1742

29 Witnesseth that the said AMBROSE JOSHUA SMITH for and in consideration of the sum of [blank] pounds current money of Virginia to him in hand paid by the said BENJAMIN HENSON the receipt whereof he doth hereby acknowledge hath granted bargained sold aliened enfeo and confirmed and by these presents doth grant bargain sell alien enfeo and confirm unto the said BENJAMIN HENSON his heirs and assigns two hundred acres of land as the same is already laid of lying one both sides of Ash branch one the upper side of Potties Creek fifty acres whereof is part of twelve hundred granted to the said AMBROSE JOSHUA SMITH by patented granted [blank] day of [blank] and the remainder hundred and fifty acres is part of an inclusive patent for fore thousand three hundred and seventy two acres granted to the said SMITH the [blank] day of June one thousand seven hundred and forty one the said Tract or parcel of land above mentioned and all and singular the premises with the appurtenances unto the said BENJAMIN HENSON and his heirs to the only use of the said BENJAMIN HENSON and of his heirs and assigns forever And the said AMBROSE JOSHUA SMITH for himself his heirs Executors Administrators doth covenant and grant to and with the said BENJAMIN HENSON his heirs and assigns by these presents that he the said AMBROSE JOSHUA SMITH now is and standeth lawfully and rightfully seised of and in the said two hundred acres of land and premises with all the appurtenances of a good perfect absolute and indefeasible estate in fee simple and now hath good right power and lawful and absolute authority to grant and convey the same according to the purport true intent and meaning of these presents and that it shall and may be lawful to and for the said BENJAMIN HENSON his heirs and assigns from time to time and at all times forever

hereafter peaceably and quietly to have and to hold occupy poses and convey the said two hundred acres of land and all and singular other the premises herein before mentioned and intended to be hereby Granted with their appur

p. Louisa County Deed Book A 14th February 1742
30 tenances without the Lett suit Trobil or interruption of him the said AMBROSE JOSHUA SMITH his heirs and assigns or any other person or persons whatsoever discharged of and from all incumbrances or Euialions whatsoever the Quitrent from henceforth to grow due to our Sovereign Lord the King only excepted foreprized And the said AMBROSE JOSHUA SMITH for himself his heirs Executors and Administrators the said two hundred acres of Land above mentioned and premises with their appurtenances unto the said BENJAMIN HENSON and his heirs against him the said AMBROSE JOSHUA SMITH his heirs and all claiming or to claim right in by from or under him or them or any of them or any other person or persons whatsoever shall and will warrant and forever defend by these presents In Witness whereof the said AMBROSE JOSHUA SMITH to these presents hath interchangeably set his hand and fixed his seal the day and year above written.

A.J. SMITH [seal]

A Memorandum that peaceabl and quiet possession of the within mentioned premises was had and taken by the within named AMBROSE JOSHUA SMITH and by him delivered to the within named BENJAMIN HENSON to be by him held according to the within written Indenture. A.J. SMITH

At a Court held for Louisa County on Monday the 14th day of February 1742.

This Indenture and Memorandum of Livery of Seisin were acknowledged by AMBROSE JOSHUA SMITH one of the parties Also JUDITH the wife of the said AMBROSE [being first privily examined] relinquished her right and title of Dower of in and unto the Lands and appurtenances therein mentioned and Ordered to be Recorded.

Test JAMES LITTLEPAGE, Clerk
Truly Recorded by LITTLEPAGE, Clk.

p. Louisa County Deed Book A 14th March 1742
31 -This Indenture made the Fourteenth day of March in the sixteenth year of the reign of Our Sovereign Lord George the second by the grace of God of Great Britain France and Ireland King Defender of the Faith &c. Anno q Dom 1742. Between CHARLES LEMAY of the County of Hanover planter of the one part and THOMAS UNDERWOOD of the County of King William of the other part. Witnesseth that the said CHARLES LEMAY for and in consideration of the sum of twenty pounds current money of Virginia to him in hand paid by the said THOMAS UNDERWOOD the receipt whereof he doth hereby acknowledge and himself there with fully satisfied contented and paid hath granted bargained sold aliened enfeoffed and confirmed and by these presents doth grant bargain sell alien enfeoffe and confirm unto the said THOMAS UNDERWOOD his heirs and assigns a certain Tract or parcel of land lying and being part thereof in the County of Hanover and the other part being the great or part in the County of Louisa containing by estimation one hundred acres be the

same more or less and is bounded by the Lands of RICHARD RICHARDSON, WILLIAM BORNE and JOHN MCGURRY which said tract or parcel of land was purchased by PETER LEMAY deceased father of the said CHARLES party to these presents and upon the death of the said PETER descended to him the said CHARLES LEMAY and all the Estate Right Title interest property claim and demand of him the said CHARLES LEMAY of in and unto the premises and the Reversion and reversions Remainder and remainders yearly and other rent and profits of the premises and of every part and parcel thereof To Have and To Hold the said Tract or parcel of Land as above bounded and all and singular the premises with the appurtenances unto the said THOMAS UNDERWOOD and his heirs to the only proper use and behoof forever and the said CHARLES LEMAY for him his heirs Exors. and Admors. doth covenant and grant to and with the said THOMAS UNDERWOOD his heirs and assigns by these presents that he the said

p. <u>Louisa County Deed Book A 14th March 1742</u>

32 CHARLES LEMAY now is and standeth Lawfully and rightfully seised of and in the said one hundred acres of Land and premises with their appurtenances of a good pure perfect absolute and indefeasible Estate in fee simple and now hath good right full power and Lawful right and absolute authority to grant and convey the same according to the purported true intent and meaning of these presents and that it shall and may be lawful to and for the said THOMAS UNDERWOOD his heirs and assigns from time to time and at all times forever hereafter peaceably and quietly to have and to hold occupy possess and enjoy the said one hundred acres of Land and all and singular other the premises herein before mentioned and intended to be hereby Granted with their appurtenances without the Lott Suit Trouble Eviction Molestation or Interruption of him the said CHARLES LEMAY his heirs or assigns or any other person or persons whatsoever discharged of and from all incumbrances whatsoever [the Dower of SARAH LEMAY widow of the said PETER LEMAY Excepted] the quitrents from hence fourth to grow due and payable to our Sovereign Lord the King his heirs and Successors only Excepted and foreprized and the said CHARLES LEMAY for himself his heirs Exors. and Admors. the said one hundred acres of land above bounded and premises with their appurtenances unto the said THOMAS UNDERWOOD and his heirs and all claiming or to claim right on by from or under him them or any of them or any other person or persons whatsoever shall and will warrant [ditto marks] and forever defend by these presents In Witness whereof the said CHARLES LEMAY to these presents hath set his hand and seal the day and year above written. CHARLES X [his mark] LEMAY [seal]

Seald & Delivered in the presence of

ABRAHM. VENABLE, JOHN CARR, RICHD. BAXTER

Memorandum that full peaceable & quiet possession & Seisen of the within mentioned Lands & premises was had & taken by the within mentioned CHARLES LEMAY & by him Delivered to the within named THOMAS UNDERWOOD and meaning to be by him according to the intent and meaning of the within written Indenture this XIV Day of March 1742.

p. Louisa County Deed Book A 14th March 1742
33 in presence of ABRAHM. VENABLE CHARLES C [his mark] LEMAY [seal]
JOHN CARR, RICHD. BAXTER

Received the XIV day of March MDCCXL of the within mentioned THOMAS UNDERWOOD the sum of twenty pounds current money the consideration within mentioned.

Test ABRAHM. VENABLE CHARLES C [his mark] LEMAY [seal]
JOHN CARR, RICHD. BAXTER

At a Court held for Louisa County on Monday the 14th of March 1742.
This Indenture receipt and memorandum of Livery and Seisen was acknowledged by CHARLES LEMAY one of the parties and Ordered to be Recorded.

Test LITTLEPAGE, Clk.
Truly Recorded by LITTLEPAGE, Clk

-I know all men by these presents that I NICHOLAS MERRIWITHER of St. James Parish in Goochland County in Virginia do for Divers good causes and consideration me thereunto moving but more especially for the Paturnall Love and affection that I bear unto my loving Grand son JOHN MERRIWITHER the son of NATHAM MERRIWITHER do give grant and confirm unto the said JOHN MERRIWITHER my Grandson two thousand acres of Land it being part of a greater tract in Louisa County Pattant bearing date the ninth day of July one thousand seven hundred and thirty. Beginning at the Dest. NICHOLAS MERRIWITHERs House at POINTERs in the Old line thence along the same North fifty degrees East one hundred and seventy poles to a corner two pines

p. Louisa County Deed Book A 14th March 1742
34 on the side of a small branch thence along another old line North forty three and a half degrees East one hundred and forty poles to POYNTORs in a vally thence a on a new line North forty degrees west one thousand and twelve poles to a corner a spanish and two chesnut oaks marked two ways in the old line thence along the same south fifty degrees west three hundred and ten poles to the above named NICHOLAS MERRIWITHER Desd. Corner two white and one Read Oak thence along the said NICHOLAS's line south forty degrees west one thousand and thirty seven poles to the beginning unto him the said JOHN his heirs and assigns forever and I do oblige my self my heirs &c. to make him a more ample Deed when there unto Required in Witness whereof I have here unto set my hand and seal this the 7th January 1742.

Signed Sealed in the presence of us
PET. JEFFERSON, THOS. MERRIWETHER NICHOLAS MERRIWETHER [seal]
ROB. LEWIS, SAMUEL DALTON

At a Court held for Louisa County on Monday the 14th day of February 1742.
This Indenture being produced in Court THOMAS MERIWETHER Gent one of the Witnesses thereto made oath that he saw NICHOLAS MERIWETHER one of the parties seal and deliver the same as his Act and Deed which is ordered to be certified.

Test JAMES LITTLEPAGE, Clk.

At a Court held for Louisa County on Monday the 14th day

p. Louisa County Deed Book A 14th March 1742
35 of March 1742.

This Indenture was further proved by the oaths of ROBERT LEWIS Gent and SAMUEL DALTON two of the Witnesses thereto and Ordered to be Recorded.

Test JAMES LITTLEPAGE, Clk.
Truly recorded by JAS. LITTLEPAGE, Clk.

-This Indenture made this twelf day of March in the year of our Lord 1742 by and between FRS. SMITHSON of the one part and SALEM BACOCK of the other part. Witnesseth that the said SMITHSON for and in consideration of the sum of five pounds current money of Virginia to him in hand already paid and received hath given granted and by these presents doth absolutely aleane the use of and grant unto the said BACOCK his heirs and assigns for ever one hundred acres of land lying and being on both sides CHAMBERLAINS Creek beginning at a corner pine on the south side of CHAMBERLAINS Creek thence north thirty degrees East seventy the aforesaid Creak & and up the same by the Water courses in all 120 poles to a corner white oake thence North fifty two degrees West to PATRICKs corner thence along PATRICKs dividing line to a corner in JOHN SMITHSONs line thence south sixty two degrees to the said SMITHSONs line to the first station with all and singular the members wrights and heridatements and appurtenances whatsoever together with all and every Deed wrighting and Evidence to the said 100 acres of Land be the same more or less according to the bounds thereof or to any part or parcel thereof in any wise appertaining to have and to hold the said 100 acres of Land and all and singular other the premises unto the said BACOCK his heirs and assigns forever and that in as firm ample manner to all intents and purposes as

p. Louisa County Deed Book A 14th March 1742
36 an estate in fee simple absolutely can be held or injoyed and shuch an estate in and for the premises the said SMITHSON binds and Obliges himself his heirs and assigns by this Deede to warrant and forever defend to be good and vallud unto the said BACOCK his heirs and assigns forever against all manner of persons claiming and any pretence wright title whatsoever And also that the said SMITHSON his heirs and assigns shall execute such other deedes and Asshurances for the better conveying the premises by the true meaning of this Deede unto the said BACOCK his heirs and assigns forever as by him them or their council shall required And to the pun Tial performance here keeping and fulfolling all and singular the premises artikals clauses and conditions of the said Deed the said SMITHSON binds and obliges himself his hers Executors Administrators and assigns in the penal sum of Two hundred pounds current money of Virginia In Witness whereof the said SMITHSON hath hearunto sett his hand and seale the day and year above written.

Signed sealed & delivered in the presence of us
JAMES LASLEY, JN. SMITHSON FR. SMITHSON [seal]

Memoradum that upon the twelf day of March 1742 full peaceable possession and seizen was given and delivered by the within named SMITHSON of the within mentioned 100 acres of Land and the appurtenances their unto belonging unto the within named for and unto the use of him his heirs and assigns for ever and the true purporte of this present Indenture.

In the presence of us JAMES LASLEY, JHN. SMITHSON FR. SMITHSON

p. Louisa County Deed Book A 14th March 1742

37 At a Court held for Louisa County on Monday the 14th of March 1742.

This Indenture and Memorandum thereon endorsed were acknowledged by FRANCIS SMITHSON one of the parties, Also SARAH the wife of the said FRANCIS [being first privily examined] relinquished all her right of Title of Dower of in and unto the Lands and appurtenances mentioned and Ordered to be Recorded.

Test JAMES LITTLEPAGE, Clerk
Truly Recorded by JAMES LITTLEPAGE, Clerk

-This Indenture made the first day of February 1742 by and between JOHN MICHIE of Hanover County of the one part and BENJAMIN ARNOLL of Louisa County of the other part Witnesseth the said JOHN MICHIE for the valliable consideration of twenty five pounds current money of Virginia to him in hand paid before the ensealing and delivery of these presents the receipt whereof I do hereby acknowledge himself to be fully satisfied contented and paid And by these presents have given granted bargained sold alienated enfeoffed and confirmed And doth by these presents fully clearly and absolutely give grant bargain sell alien enfeoffe and confirm unto the said BENJAMIN ARNOLL his heirs executors administrators and assigns for ever one parcel of land containing Two hundred acres more or less situate lying and being in the forks of Pamunkey river ajoining to the lands of GEORGE ALVES, THOMAS HENDERSON and ALEXANDER CARR which said Two hundred acres of Land above said is part and parcel of Four hundred acres which the said JOHN MICHIE hath obtained a patent for the said land being in the parish of Saint Martins in the County of Louisa To have and to hold the above granted premises with all and singular its rights members jurisdictions

p. Louisa County Deed Book A 14th March 1742

38 and appurtenances together with all houses buildings gardens orchards lands meadows feedings paustures woods and underwoods waterways profits and comoditys whatsoever thereupon or thereunto belonging or in any wise appertaining unto the said BENJAMIN ARNOLL his heirs and assigns forever And the said JOHN MICHIE doe for himself his heirs and assigns covenant grant and agree to and with the said BENJAMIN ARNOLL his heirs and assigns in manner and form following [Viz.] that he the said BENJAMIN ARNOLL his heirs and assigns may and shall from time to time and at all times for ever hereafter peaceably and quietly have hold use occupy posses and enjoy the above granted premises and every part and parcell with every of their Rights members Jurisdictions and appurtenances and have receive and take the uses profits and comodityes to his or their

proper uses and behoofs for ever without any Lawfull suit trouble denial Eviction or disturbance of him the said JOHN MICHIE or his heirs Executors Administrators or of any person or persons whatsoever by from or under him them or any of them or by their or any of their means Act priority or procurement And the said JOHN MICHIE doe for himself his heirs and assigns further covenant promise grant and agree to and with the said BENJAMIN ARNOLL his heirs and assigns to serve and defend the above granted premises with their and every of their Rights members Jurisdictions and appurtenances unto the said BENJAMIN ARNOLL his heirs and assigns forever to be free and clear and freely and clearly acquitted and exonerated and discharged and from all manner of former and other Gifts Grants Bargains Sales Seals Thirds Dowries and all other incumbrances whatsoever And lastly the said JOHN MICHIE doth further covenant promise and agree to and with the said BENJAMIN ARNOLL his heirs and assigns to make doe perform and accomplish or cause to be made done performed and accomplished all and every other Act and Acts thing and things device

p. Louisa County Deed Book A 14th March 1742

39 and devices whatsoever in the Law for the strengthening and confirming the premises be it by Deed or Deeds or by any other way or means which shall by the said BENJAMIN ARNOLL his heirs or assigns or by his or their Council learned in the Law be reasonable advised devised or required as witness whereof I have hereunto set my hand and seal the day and year above written.

Signed Sealed & Delivered in presence of us

JOHN HARLOW, THOMAS HARLOW, ANN HARLOW JOHN MICHIE [seal]

Memorandum that quiet and peaceable possession was granted of the within mentioned Land and premises to BENJAMIN ARNOLL by the other party Covenantor to these presents.

In presence of us

JOHN HARLOW, THOMAS HARLOW, ANN HARLOW JOHN MICHIE

At a Court held for Louisa County on Monday the 14th day of March 1742.

This Indenture and Memorandum thereon endorsed were acknowledged by JOHN MICHIE one of the parties and Ordered to be recorded.

Test JAMES LITTLEPAGE, Clk.

Truly Recorded by JAMS. LITTLEPAGE, Clerk

-This Indenture made the fourteenth day of March in the year of our Lord one thousand seven hundred and forty two Between RANDOLPH BOBIT of the County of Louisa Carpender of the one part and PHILIP REYNOLDS of the County of Louisa a planter of the other part. The said RANDOLPH BOBIT in consideration of Eight pounds current money to

p. Louisa County Deed Book A 14th March 1742

40 him in hand paid by the said PHILIP REYNOLDS before sealing and delivery of these presents the receipt whereof the said RANDOLPH BOBIT doth hereby acknowledge hath granted bargained sold aliened enfeoffed and confirmed and by these presents doth grant bargain sell alien enfeoff and confirm unto the said PHILIP REYNOLDS his heirs and

assigns Two hundred acres of Land lying and being in Louisa County and on the South fork of FOSTERs Creek and part of a greater Track that was granted to the said RANDOLPH BOBIT of the aforesaid County and bounded as followeth Beginning on the corner stake in JOHN PRINCES line runing thence to POINTERs the said PRINCES line thence to a corner white oake in PRICES line thence to a corner pine in CHARLES MOORMENs line thence to a corner oak and pine in the said MOORMANs line thence to POINTERs which are three pines and thence to the first station. And all woods ways waters profits and emoluments whatsoever to the said Track of Land belonging or appertaining and the reversions and remainders thereof and every part and parsell thereof and all the estate right title and interest whatsoever of him the said RANDOLPH BOBIT in and to the said Bargained promises and appurtenances and every part and parsell thereof to have and to hold the said Track of Land and all and singular the premises with the appurtenances unto the said PHILIP REYNOLDS his heirs and assigns for ever to the only proper use and behoof of him the said PHILIP REYNOLDS his heirs and assigns forever And the said RANDOLPH BOBIT for himself his heirs Executors and Administrators doth by these presents Covenant promise and agree to and with the said PHILIP REYNOLDS that he the said RANDOLPH BOBIT at the time of sealing

p. <u>Louisa County Deed Book A 14th March 1742</u>
41 and delivery of these presents is and stands seised of and indefeasible Estate of Inheritance in fee simple in the said Land premises and hath clear absolute full right and authority to sell and convey the same in manner and form aforesaid and the said PHILIP REYNOLDS his heirs and assigns shall and may for ever hereafter peaceably and quietly have hold process and Injoy all and singular the premises and appurtenances without Let suit or Molestation of any person whatsoever having or Lawfully claiming and Estate Right or title or to the same or any part thereof and the said RANDOLPH BOBIT and his heirs shall and will warrant and for ever defend by these presents the aforesaid Tract of land and premises with the appurtenances unto the said PHILLIP REYNOLDS his heirs and assigns against him the said RANDOLPH BOBIT and his heirs and all and any other person or persons having or lawfully claiming any Estate right or title to the same or any part of parcell thereof In Witness whereof the said parties have hereunto interchangeably set their hands and affixed their seals the day and year above written.

Seal'd and delivered in presence of

JAMES BUCHANAN, JOHN DAVIS RANDOLPH BOBIT [seal]

Received of PHILLIP REYNOLDS eight pounds current money the following consideration within mentioned March 14th 1742.

JAMES BUCHANAN, JOHN DAVIS RANDOLPH BOBIT

Memorandum that on this fourteenth day of March Livery and Seisen of the within Bargained Land and premises with the

p. <u>Louisa County Deed Book A 14th March 1742</u>
42 appurtenances was made by me RANDOLPH BOBIT unto the said PHILLIP REYNOLDS his heirs and assigns forever according to the form and effect of within Indenture.

In presence of JAMES BUCHANAN, JOHN DAVIS RANDOLPH BOBIT
At a Court held for Louisa County on Monday the 14th day of March 1742.
This Indenture receipt and Memorandum of Livery and Seisen were acknowledged by RANDOLPH BOBIT one of the parties and ordered to be recorded.

Test JAMES LITTLEPAGE, Clk.
Truly Recorded by JAS. LITTLEPAGE, Clk.

-This Indenture made the Twelveth day of March in the year of our Lord one thousand seven hundred and forty two Between WILLIAM COURSEY planter of the one part & ABRAHAM ALLEN planter of the other part Witnesseth that the said WILLIAM COURSEY for and in consideration of the sum of twelve pounds current money of Virginia to him in hand paid by the said ABRAHAM ALLEN at & before the ensealing & delivery of these presents Hath given granted bargained sold aliened released & confirmed And by these presents doth give grant bargain sell alien release and confirm unto the ABRAHAM ALLEN all that his piece or parcel of land situate lying & being in the County of Louisa & Fredericksvile parish between the two ridges of Mountains containing Two hundred acres be the same more or less lying and being on the south side of Piney Mountain and being part of four hundred acres patented by the said WILLIAM COURSEY and Bounded as follows, Beginning at COURSEY's several oak bushes runing

p. <u>Louisa County Deed Book A 14th March 1742</u>

43 thence North thirty degrees East one hundred and forty poles to a pine thence fifty degrees East to several marked pines in a stony piece of Ground near the East side of a Branch in the said COURSEY's line and along the same South thirteen degrees West two hundred and ten poles to his corner stake in another line of his & along the same North thirty degrees West two hundred and four poles to the first station, Together with all the houses orchards gardens and all other improvements whatsoever and also all the woods underwoods waies waters and water COURSEY's and all other profits comodities and advantages to the same belonging or in any wise appertaining To Have and To Hold the plantation Land and house all & singular other the premises with their and every of their appurtenances unto the said ABRAHAM ALLEN his heirs and assigns forever to the said WILLIAM COURSEY for him and his heirs executors administrators doth covenant, grant and agree to and with the said ABRAHAM ALLEN his heirs executors Administrators and assigns in manner and form following [that is to say] that he the said WILLIAM COURSEY at the time of the ensealing and delivery hereof is and stands lawfully seized of an absolute and indefeasible Estate of Inheritance in fee simple of and in the Land and other premises herein before conveyed and every part and parcel thereof and hath good right title and lawful authority to grant bargain and sell the same in manner aforesaid. And that the said ABRAHAM ALLEN his heirs and assigns shall and may from time to time and at all times hereafter quietly and peaceably have hold possess and enjoy the above granted lands and premises and every part and parcel thereof with the appurtenances without any Lawful Let Suit Trouble Eviction or Molestation of him the said WILLIAM COURSEY his heirs or assigns

or any other person or persons whatsoever claiming or to claim by from or under him them or any of them and that free & clear and freely and clearly acquited and discharged or by the said WILLIAM COURSEY his heirs Executors Admrs. or some of them from time to time

p. Louisa County Deed Book A 14th March 1742
44 and at all times hereafter kept harmless and Indimetied of and from all & all manner of former and other bargains sales gifts grants Intailes Dowers & Titles of Dower & all other charge & incumbrances whatsoever had made commited done or suffered by him the said WILLIAM COURSEY or by any other person or persons whatsoever Claiming or to claim from or under him And Lastly the said WILLIAM COURSEY the said Land & premises hereof before bargained & sold with their and every of the appurtenances unto the said ABRAHAM ALLEN and to his heirs or assigns will warrant and forever defend by these presents In Witness whereof the parties to these presents his hand and seal have set the day of the year first above written. Signed Sealed and Delivered

in presence of WILLIAM W [his mark] COREY [seal]

JOHN HACKETT, JOHN STAPLES

Received the twelveth day of March one thousand seven hundred and forty two the sum of twelve pounds current money of Virginia being the consideration money within mentioned I say Rec'd of ABRAHAM ALLEN to me. WILLIAM W [his mark] COURSEY [seal]

At a Court held for Louisa County on 14th day of March 1742.

This Indenture and receipt thereon indorsed were acknowledged by WILLIAM COURSEY one of the parties and Ordered to be Recorded.

Test JAMES LITTLEPAGE, Clk.

Truly Recorded by JAS. LITTLEPAGE, Clk.

-This Indenture made this fourteenth day of March in the fifteenth year of the Reign of our Sovereign Lord George the Second by the Grace of God of Great Britain France and Ireland King Defender of the Faith &c.

p. Louisa County Deed Book A 14th March 1742
45 and in the year of our Lord Christ one thousand seven hundred and forty two Between PETER GARLAND, JUN. of Hanover County and ROBERT GARLAND of Louisa County of the one part and BENJAMIN DUMAS of the said County of Louisa of the other part. Witnesseth that the said PETER and ROBERT GARLAND for and in consideration of the sum of Thirty Eight pounds Eight shillings and five pence current money of Virginia to them in hand paid by the said BENJAMIN DUMAS at and before the ensealing and delivery of these presents the receipt whereof they do hereby acknowledge and thereof and of every part and parcel of the same do clearly acquit and discharge the said BENJAMIN DUMAS his Executors and Administrators and every of them by these presents, Have given Granted Aliened Bargained Sold Enfeoffed and Confirmed And by these presents do fully clearly and absolutely give grant alien bargain sell enfeoff and purposely confirm unto the said ROBERT GARLAND their tract or parcel of land containing one hundred acres more or less

situate lying and being in the aforesaid County of Louisa on the North side of Little River and is bounded as followeth [to wit] Beginning at an Elm and Hickory saplin on the North side of the River runing thence North forty eight degrees East one hundred and eighteen poles to two red oaks thence south forty degrees East ninety eight poles to a hiccory thence south sixty one degrees East thirty four poles to three red oake and a hiccory corner of SAMUEL GOODMAN's thence along his line South sixty one and a half degrees West One hundred & thirty seven poles to a Corner Maple on the River Bend thence up the said River by the several meanders thereof to the beginning which said one hundred acres of Land above bounded is the moiety of a greater Tract granted by patent bearing date the 20th day of February 1719 to JOHN GARLAND late of Hanover County deceased and by his last Will and Testament the same was left to be divided between the said PETER and ROBERT GARLAND, With all and

p. Louisa County Deed Book A 14th March 1742

46 singular its rights members Jurisdictions and appurtenances with all Houses Edifices buildings Gardens Orchards Yards Land Tenements Meadows feedings pastures woods underwoods ways easments profits and commodities hereditaments and appurtenances whatsoever to the said land and premises or to any part or parcel of the same belonging or in any wise appertaining and the Reversion and Reversions Remainder and remainders of all and singular the before mentioned premises with their and every of their appurtenances and also all the Estate Right Title Interest possession property Claim and demand whatsoever of them the said PETER and ROBERT GARLAND in or to the same or any part thereof To Have and To Hold the said one hundred acres of Land above bounded be the same more or less and all and singular the presents hereby Granted Bargained Sold or intended to be herein or hereafter Granted Bargained & Sold with their and every of their Right members and appurtenances whatsoever unto the said BENJAMIN DUMAS his heirs and assigns forever And they the said PETER and ROBERT GARLAND for themselves their heirs Executors and all other persons the said Lands and all and singular the premises before Granted and Sold with all appurtenances unto the said BENJAMIN DUMAS and his heirs to the only proper use of the said BENJAMIN DUMAS his heirs and assigns forever against them the said PETER and ROBERT GARLAND their heirs and assigns and all and every person or persons whatsoever shall and will warrant forever and defend by these presents And lastly they the said PETER and ROBERT GARLAND for themselves their heirs Executors & Administrators doth covenant and grant to and with the said BENJAMIN DUMAS his heirs and assigns and every of them by these presents that they the said PETER and ROBERT GARLAND their heirs and all and every other person or persons Lawfully claiming or rightfully pretending to have or which hereafter shall have any Estate Right Title Interest or demand of in or unto the

p. Louisa County Deed Book A 14th March 1742

47 premises or any part or parcel of them by from or under the said PETER and ROBERT GARLAND them their heirs or assigns shall and will from time to time and at all times

for ever hereafter and upon the reasonable request and at the costs and charges in the Law of the said BENJAMIN DUMAS his heirs and assigns make do perform acknowledge levy execute or suffer or excuse to be made done performed acknowledged levyed executed and suffered all and every such further Lawful and reasonable Act and Acts thing or things devices or devices assurance and assurances conveyance and conveyances in the Law whatsoever for the further better and more perfect assurance surity sure making and conveying all and singular the before mentioned premises and every of their Rights members and appurtenances unto the said BENJAMIN DUMAS his heirs and assigns forever as by the said BENJAMIN DUMAS or by his or their Council learned in the Law shall be reasonably devised advised or required. In Witness whereof the parties to these presents their hands and seals have interchangeably set and affixed the day and year first above written.

Signed sealed & delivered
in the presence of
JN. PRYOR, HUM. GAINES
GEORGE THOMPSON

PETER GARLAND [seal]
ROBERT GARLAND [seal]

Memorandum That on the day and year within written peaceable and quiet possession of the Land and premises within granted and sold was had and taken by the within named PETER and ROBERT GARLAND and by them delivered over to the within named BENJAMIN DUMAS to hold to him his heirs and assigns for ever according to the purport true intent and meaning of the within mentioned Indenture.

In presence of
JN. PRYOR, HUM. GAINES,
GEORGE THOMPSON

PETER GARLAND [seal]
ROBERT GARLAND [seal]

p. Louisa County Deed Book A 14th March 1742

48 Received the 14th day of March 1742 of BENJAMIN DUMAS the sum of Thirty eight pounds eight shillings and five pence current money of Virginia being the consideration for the Land and premises within Granted and sold by the within named PETER and ROBERT GARLAND unto the said BENJAMIN DUMAS and his heirs forever according to the effect of these Indenture.

PETER GARLAND ROBERT GARLAND

At a Court held for Louisa County on Monday the 14th day of March 1742.
This Indenture Receipt Memorandum of Livery and Seisen were acknowledged by PETER GARLAND and ROBERT GARLAND parties and ordered to be recorded.

Test JAMES LITTLEPAGE, Clk
Truly Recorded by JAM. LITTLEPAGE, Clk.

-This Indenture made the fourteenth day of March in the year of our Lord One thousand seven hundred and forty two Between WILLIAM BUNCH and HENRY BUNCH of the one part and JOHN BUNCH of the other part. Witnesseth that the said WILLIAM BUNCH and HENRY BUNCH for and in consideration of fifteen pounds current money of Virginia to them in hand paid That is to say the sum of seven pounds ten current to WILLIAM BUNCH and seven pounds ten current to HENRY BUNCH to them in hand paid by the said JOHN BUNCH at and before the ensealing and delivery of these presents the receipt whereof the said WILLIAM BUNCH and HENRY BUNCH doth hereby confess and acknowledge Hath given Granted Bargained Sold Aliened Released and confirmed and by these presents

p. Louisa County Deed Book A 14th March 1742

49 doth give grant bargain sell alien release and confirm unto the said JOHN BUNCH all that their parts and parcels of Lands situate lying and being in the County of Louisa & Fredrickvile parish containing by estimation one hundred and twenty acres [that is to say Sixty acres from WILLIAM BUNCH and sixty acres from HENRY BUNCH which is part of a survey of four hundred acres patented by JOHN BUNCH deceased and by the last Will and Testament of the said JOHN BUNCH deceased left one hundred acres of Land including the plantation unto this purchaser his son JOHN BUNCH and the remainder to be equally divided Between WILLIAM BUNCH, HENRY BUNCH, DAVID BUNCH and JAMES BUNCH &c. also his sons] which said parts of WILLIAM BUNCH and HENRY BUNCH parts laid of out of the Tract above mentioned which said parts are by these presents sold unto JOHN BUNCH & his heirs forever together with all houses orchards gardens and all other improvements whatsoever And also all woods underwoods ways waters and watercourses and all other profits comodities and advantages to the same belonging or in any wise appertaining To Have and to hold the said lands and all and singular the premises with their and every of their appurtenances unto the said JOHN BUNCH his heirs and assigns forever to the said WILLIAM BUNCH and HENRY BUNCH for themselves their heirs Executors and Admrs. doth covenant grant and agree to and with the said JOHN BUNCH his heirs Executors Admrs. and assigns in manner and form following [that is to say] that they the said WILLIAM BUNCH and HENRY BUNCH at the time of the ensealing and delivery hereof is and lands lawfully seized of an absolute & indefeasable Estate of Inheritance in fee simple of and in the Land and other the

p. Louisa County Deed Book A 14th March 1742

50 premises herein before conveyed and every part and parcel thereof and hath good right title and Lawfull authority to grant bargain and sell the same in manner aforesaid and that the said JOHN BUNCH his heirs and assigns shall and may from time to time and at all times hereafter quietly and peaceably have hold possess and injoy the above granted Land and premises and every part and parcel thereof with the appurtenances without any Lawful Lott Suit Trouble Eviction or Molestation of them the said WILLIAM BUNCH and HENRY BUNCH their heirs or assigns or any other person or persons whatsoever claiming or claim by from or under them or either of them And that free and clear and freely and clearly acquited & discharged or by the said WILLIAM BUNCH and HENRY BUNCH their heirs Executors Administrators or some of them from time to time and at all times hereafter kept harmless & indemnified of and from all and all manner and former and other Bargain Sales Gifts Grants intails Dowers & titles of Dower and all other charge and imcumbrances whatsoever had made comitted done or suffered by them the said WILLIAM BUNCH and HENRY BUNCH or by and other person or persons whatsoever claiming or to claim by from or

under them or either of them And Lastly the said WILLIAM BUNCH and HENRY BUNCH the said Lands and premises herein before bargained and sold with their and every of their appurtenances unto the said JOHN BUNCH his heirs and assigns will warrant and for ever defend by these presents. In Witness whereof the parties to these presents their hand & seals have set the day of the year first above written.

Sign'd seal'd & deliver'd
in presence of HENRY BUNCH [seal]
A.J. SMITH, BENJ. HENSLEE WILLIAM BUNCH [seal]

Enter Lined before assigned betwix the third and forth line the word tenn again the same word betwix the forth and fifth line.

p. Louisa County Deed Book A 14th March 1742
51 Memorandum that peaceable and quiet possession of the within mentioned premises was first had and taken by the within named WILLIAM BUNCH and HENRY BUNCH and by them delivered to the within named JOHN BUNCH to be by him held according to the within written Indenture.

In presence of HENRY BUNCH
A.J. SMITH, BENJ. HENSLEE WILLIAM BUNCH

Rec'd of JOHN BUNCH the fourteenth day of March one thousand seven hundred and forty two the sum of fifteen pounds current money of Virginia being the consideration money within mentioned and received of JOHN BUNCH of us. HENRY BUNCH WILLIAM BUNCH
At a Court held for Louisa County the 14th day of March 1742.
This Indenture Receipt and Memorandum of Livery and Seisen were acknowledged by HENRY BUNCH and WILLIAM BUNCH parties thereunto and Ordered to be recorded.

Test JAMES LITTLEPAGE, Clk.
Truly recorded by JAM. LITTLEPAGE, Clerl

-This Indenture made this fourteenth day of March in the year of our Lord Christ one thousand seven hundred and fourty two Between JOHN MORRIS of St. Martins parish in the County of Louisa of the one part and ARCHELAUS YANCEY of the aforesaid County and parish of the other part. Witnesseth that the said JOHN MORRIS for and in consideration of the sum of twelve pounds current money of Virginia to him in hand paid by the said

p. Louisa County Deed Book A 14th March 1742
52 ARCHELAUS YANCEY at and before the ensealing and delivery of these presents the receipt whereof he doth hereby acknowledge and thereof and of every part and parcel of the same doth clearly acquit and discharge the said ARCHELAUS YANCEY his Executors and Administrators and every of them by these presents Hath granted aliened released enfeoffed and confirmed and by these presents for the consideration above set down Doth grant alien release enfeoffe and perpetually confirm unto the said ARCHELAUS YANCEY and to his heirs and assigns for ever Eighty acres of Land lying & being on the upper side of a branch of the Little River called the Horse Pen swamp in the aforesaid parish and

County be the same more or less within the bounds hereafter set down [to wit] begining at a stooping Ash in the said ARCHELAUS YANCEYs line on the Horse pen swamp thence up the said swamp to a large poper at the mouth of small branch thence up the said branch to a corner black oak in JOSEPH BICKLEYs line thence along the said BICKLEYs line to a corner red oak saplin standing in the aforesaid ARCHELAUS YANCEYs line thence along the said ARCHELAUS YANCEYs line to the begining, And all the Estate Rights Title Interest use property and Claim of him the said JOHN MORRIS of in or unto the premises and the reversion and reversions remainder and remainders yearly and other rents and profits of the premises and of every part and parcell thereof To Have and To Hold the Eighty acres of land above bounded be the same more or less and all and singular other the premises herein before mentioned and intended to be hereby granted with there and every of there appurtenances unto the said ARCHELAUS YANCEY and of his heirs and assigns for ever And the said JOHN MORRIS for himself his heirs Exors. and Admrs. doth covenant and grant to and with the said ARCHELAUS YANCEY his heirs and assigns by these presents that he the said JOHN MORRIS now

p. Louisa County Deed Book A 14th March 1742

53 and standeth lawfully and rightfully seized of and in the said eighty acres of land be the same more or less as aforesaid and premises with the appurtenances of a good sure perfect absolute indefeasible Estate in fee simple and now hath good right full power and lawful and absolute authority to grant and convey the same according to the purport true intent & meaning of these presents And that it shall and may be lawfull to and for the said ARCHELAUS YANCEY his heirs and assigns from time to time and at all times forever hereafter peaceably quietly to have hold and occupy possess and enjoy the said eighty acres of land above bounded by the same more or less said is and all and singular other the premises herein before mentioned and intended to be hereby granted with their and every of their appurtenances without any lawful lot suite troble or interruption of him the said JOHN MORRIS his heirs or assigns or any other person or persons whatsoever discharged of and from all incumbrances or evictions whatsoever quitrents and successors only excepted and foreprized And the said JOHN MORRIS for himself his heirs Executors and Administrators the aforesaid granted premises with their appurtenances unto the said ARCHELAUS YANCEY his heirs against him the said JOHN MORRIS and his heirs and all claiming to claim right in by from or under him them or any of them or any other person or persons whatsoever shall and will warrant and for ever defend by these presents. Witness whereof the said JOHN MORRIS to these presents hath interchangeably set his hand and affixed his seal the day and year above first written. Sined

MATH. JOUET JOHN MORRIS [seal]

JAS. GOODALL, BENJA. HENSON

Memorandum that peaceable and quiet possession of the premises within mentioned was had and taken by the within named JOHN MORRIS and by him delivered to the within named ARCHELAUS YANCEY

p. Louisa County Deed Book A 14th March 1742

54 to hold according to the within written Indenter.

Test MATH. JOUET JOHN MORRIS [seal]

JAS. GOODALL, BENJA. HENSON

At a Court held for Louisa County on Monday the 14th day of March 1742.
This Indenture and Memorandum of Livery and Seisen were acknowledged by JOHN MORRIS one of the parties and ordered to be recorded.

Test JAMES LITTLEPAGE, Clk.

Truly recorded by JAMS. LITTLEPAGE, Clk.

-This Indenture made this twelf day of March in the year of our Lord one M seven hundred and forty two By and Between FR. SMITHSON of the one part and THO. GIBSON of the other part Witnesseth that the said SMITHSON hath for and in consideration of the sum of two thousand one hundred and fifty pounds of neate bundel Tobaco to him in hand all ready paide and satisfied hath Given Granted and by these presents doth absolutely aliane the use of and Grant unto the said GIBSON his heirs and assigns forever one Water Mill together with the Mill Dam Mill Stones & Mill Iron Mill hous and all other convenancies thereunto belongin together with one Acre of Land lying on the North side of the aforesaid Mill creak and bounded as follows, to wit, Beginning at the Mill door runing thence south 76 degrees West 6 poles to 4 Maypoles joined at the rootes thence North 14 degrees West 13 poles to a stake thence North 76 degrees East 12 poles to a hickory Grub thence south 14 degrees East 13 poles into the Mill pond thence South 76 degrees West 6 poles to the beginning with all maner and all singular the members rights and heridatements and appurtenances whatsoever

p. Louisa County Deed Book A 14th March 1742

55 together with all and every Deed weighting the said Acre of Land and Mill or to any part or parcel thereof in any wise apertaining To Have and To Hold the said acre of land and Mill be the same more or less according to the bounds thereof and all and singular other the premises unto the said GIBSON his heirs and assigns forever &c. and that in as firm ample manner to all intents and purposes as & Estate in fee simple absolutely can be held and enjoyed and shuch an Estate in and for the premises the said SMITHSON binds and obliges himself his heirs and assigns by the Deed to warrant & for ever defend to be good and vallied to the said GIBSON his heirs and assigns for and against all maner of persons claiming under any pretence wrighte or titiel whatsoever and also that the said SMITHSON his heirs and assigns shall execute shuch other Deeds and asureances for the better conveying the premises by the true meaning of this Deed unto the said GIBSON his heirs and assigns forever as by him them or their council shall be required and to the puntiall performance true keeping and fulfilling of all and singular the premises artickels clausis and conditions of this Deed the said SMITHSON binds and obliges himself his heirs executors Administrators and assigns in the penial sum of Two hundred pounds current money of Virginia. In Witness whereof the said SMITHSON hath hereunto sett his hand and

seal the day and year within written.

Signed Sealed & delivered in presence of us

JOHN SMITHSON, SALEM BOCOCK FR. SMITHSON [seal]

Memorandum that upon the twelf day of March 1742 full and peasable posetion and Seizen was given and delivered by the within SMITHSON of the within mentioned Acre of Land and the aforesaid Mill apurtaining thereto with the apurtenances unto the said within named GIBSON for and unto

p. Louisa County Deed Book A 14th March 1742

56 the use of him his heirs and assigns forever according to the true purporte of this present Indenture. In the preasence of us,

JOHN SMITHSON, SALAM BOCOCK FR. SMITHSON [seal]

At a Court held for Louisa County on Monday the 14th day of March 1742.
This Indenture and Memorandum thereon endorsed were acknowledged by FRANCIS SMITHSON one of the parties, Also SARAH the wife of the said FRANCIS [she being first privily examined] relinquished all her rights and title of Dower of in and unto the Lands and appurtenances therein mentioned and Ordered to be Recorded.

Test JAMES LITTLEPAGE, Clk.
Truly recorded by JAMS. LITTLEPAGE, Clk.

-This Indenture made this fourteenth day of March in the year of our Lord Christ one thousand seven hundred and forty two Between PHILIP WILLSON of the parish of Fredericksville in the County of Louisa planter of the one part and JAMES COLEMAN of the parish of St. Thomas in the County of Orange Gent. of the other part. Witnesseth that the said PHILIP WILLSON for and in consideration of the sum of nineteen pounds ten shillings current money of Virginia to him in hand paid by the said JAMES COLEMAN the receipt whereof he doth hereby acknowledge Hath Granted Bargained Sold Aliened Enfeoffed and Confirmed and by these presents Doth Grant Bargain Sell Alien Enfeoff and Confirm unto the said JAMES COLEMAN his heirs and assigns for ever all that the said PHILIP WILLSON his parcel or Tract of land containing four hundred acres on the West side of the little Mountains in the aforesaid parish of Fredericksville and County of Louisa and is bounded as follows

p. Louisa County Deed Book A 14th March 1742

57 [to wit] Beginning at WILLIAM CRADOCK's corner red oak and two gums runing thence South thirty one degrees West at forty eight a branch in all one hundred and thirty two poles to two pines thence South fifty five degrees West one hundred and twenty poles to a white oak red oak and pine on the side of a Hill thence West at thirty eight a branch in all eighty nine poles to a white oake and red oak thence North thirty six West ninety poles to two white oaks thence North thirty and a half degrees East and twelve two more branches in all three hundred and sixty eight poles to CRADOCK's Corner red oak thence along his line South thirty one degrees East Two hundred and forty poles to the beginning which said four hundred acres of land above bounded was granted to

TIMOTHY DALTON by patent bearing date the [blank] day of [blank] and by him conveyed to the said PHILIP WILLSON by Deeds proved in Hanover County Court by JOSEPH MARTINS and AMBROSE JOSHUA SMITH two of the Witnesses thereof and all houses Marshes ways waters profills Emoluments and the appurtenances thereunto belonging and the Reversion and Reversions Remainder and Remainders thereof and of every part thereof and all the Estate right Title interest Claim and demand whatsoever of him the said PHILLIP WILLSON in and to the same To Have and To Hold the said Tract or parcell of Land and all and singular the premises with the appurtenances unto the said JAMES COLEMAN his heirs and assigns to the only use and behoof of the said JAMES COLEMAN his heirs and assigns for ever and the said PHILIP WILLSON and his heirs and all and singular the premises with the appurtenances to the

p. <u>Louisa County Deed Book A 14th March 1742</u>
58 said JAMES COLEMAN his heirs and assigns shall and will warrant and for ever defend by these presents And the said PHILIP WILLSON for himself his heirs Executors and Administrators doth Covenant and Grant to and with the said JAMES COLEMAN his heirs and assigns in manner and form following, that is to say, that he the said PHILIP WILLSON is and now stands seized of an indefeasible Estate of Fee Simple in the premises and hath good right to sell and convey the same in manner aforesaid and that the said JAMES COLEMAN his heirs and assigns of and may for ever hereafter peaceably and quietly to have hold occupy and enjoy the same premises without the Suite Let Molestation disturbance of him the said PHILIP WILLSON and his heirs or of any other person or persons having or lawfully claiming any Right or Title therein and that freed and discharged of and from all other and former Estates Rights Titles and of and from all Judgment Executions debts Mortgages and other incumbrances whatsoever the Quitrents from henceforth to grow due to our Sovereign Lord the King his heirs and successors only excepted and foreprized. In Witness whereof the said PHILIP WILLSON hath interchangeably set his hand and affixed his seal the day and year first above written.

Signed sealed & delivered
in the presence of PHILIP Q [his mark] WILLSON [seal]
A.J. SMITH, GEORGE EASTHAM, JOHN STARKE

Memorandum that peaceable and quiet possession of the premises within mentioned was had and taken by the within named PHILIP WILLSON and by him delivered to the within named JAMES COLEMAN to hold according to the within written Indenture.

A.J. SMITH, GEORGE EASTHAM, JOHN STARKE PHILIP Q [his mark] WILLSON [seal]

p. <u>Louisa County Deed Book A 14th March 1742</u>
59 At a Court held for Louisa County on Monday the 14th day of March 1742.
This Indenture and Memorandum of Livery and Seisen were acknowledged by PHILIP WILLSON one of the parties, And ordered to be recorded.

Test JAMES LITTLEPAGE, Clk.
Truly recorded by JAMS. LITTLEPAGE, Clk.

-This Indenture made the fourth day of December in the fifteenth year of the Reign of our Sovereign Lord George the second by the Grace of God of Great Britain France and Ireland King Defender of the Faith &c. and in the year of our Lord Christ MDCCXLII Between JAMES HILL of the parish of St. John in the County of King William planter of the one part and JOHN HILL of the parish of St. Martin's in the County of Louisa of the other part. Witnesseth that the said JAMES HILL for and in consideration of the sum of thirty pounds current money of Virginia to him in hand paid by the said JOHN HILL at and before the ensealing and delivery of these presents the receipt whereof the said JAMES HILL doth acknowledge and thereof and of every part and parcel thereof doth acquit and discharge the said JOHN HILL his heirs Executors Administrators and assigns by these presents Hath Given Granted Bargained Sold and by these presents for himself his heirs Executors Administrators Doth Give Grant Bargain and Sell unto the said JOHN HILL his heirs and assigns all that parcel Tract or Dividend of Land lying and being in the County of Louisa containing by Estimation Two hundred Acres be the same more or less and bounded as follows [Viz.] Begining at a Red Oak on the South side the South Anna River at the mouth of the Horse shoe Neck thence up the River by the Water

p. Louisa County Deed Book A 14th March 1742

60 courses making in a straight line one hundred and sixty five poles to a Corner a little below the mouth of a branch thence into the woods North sixty five West one hundred and ninety six poles to a Corner thence South thirty East three hundred and forty four poles to several marked trees thence North forty five East Eighty poles to the begining, which the said two hundred Acres of Land above bounded are part of four hundred acres that were granted to one JOHN SYME, Gent. by patent bearing date the seventeenth day of August in the year of our Lord Christ MDCCXXV and by the said SYME conveyed to the said WALTER CLOPTON by a Deed acknowledged in the Court of the said County of Hanover bearing date the sixth day of January in the year of our Lord Christ MDCCXXVI and by the said CLOPTON conveyed to the said JAMES HILL by a Deed acknowledged in the Court of the said County of Hanover bearing date the fourth day of October in the year of our Lord Christ MDCCXXXIV and all the Estate Right Title Interest use property claim and demand whatsoever of him the said JAMES HILL his heirs Executors Administrators or assigns of in or unto the premises or any part of parcel thereof and Reversion and Reversions Remainder and Remainders Rents Issues and profits of all and singular the above mentioned premises with their and every of their appurtenances To Have and To Hold to the said JOHN HILL his heirs and assigns to the only proper use and behoof of him the said JOHN HILL and of his heirs and assigns forever. And the said JAMES HILL for himself his heirs Exors. and Admors. doth covenant Grant and agree to and with the said JOHN HILL his heirs and assigns in manner and form following that is to say that he the said JAMES HILL now is and standeth justly and rightfully seized of the above mentioned Land and premises with the appurtenances and convey the same to the said JOHN HILL his heirs and assigns by

p. Louisa County Deed Book A 14th March 1742

61 these presents and that it shall and may be lawful to and for the said JOHN HILL his heirs and assigns from time to time and at all times for ever hereafter to have hold use Occupy possess and enjoy all and singular the above granted premises with their and every of their appurtenances free and clear of all incumbrances whatsoever [the Quitrents henceforth to be due excepted] and further that he the said JAMES HILL the above granted premises with all appurtenances unto him the said JOHN HILL and his heirs & assigns against him the said JAMES HILL his heirs Exors. and Admors. and all claiming or to Claim any Right Title or Interest to the same or any part thereof by from or under him them or any of them or by from or under any other person or person whatsoever will for ever warrant and defend by these presents. In witness whereof the parties to these presents their hands and seals interchangeably have set the day and year first above written

Signed seal'd & deliver'd JAMES HILL [seal]
in the presence of
JOHN CLARKSON, JOHN BAILEY, WILLIAM X [his mark] LONG

Received this fourth day of December MDCCXLII of JOHN HILL the sum of thirty pounds current money being the consideration money within mentioned for the Lands and premises within granted and sold according to the purport and true intent and meaning of the within Deed I say received of me. JOHN HILL

Test JOHN CLARKSON, JOHN BAILEY, WILLIAM X [his mark] LONG

Memorandum that on the day and year within mentioned peaceable and quiet possession and seizen of the Land within mentioned was has &

p. Louisa County Deed Book A 14th March 1742

62 taken by the within JAMES HILL and by him delivered unto the within named JOHN HILL according to the form and effect of the within Deed. JOHN HILL [seal]

In presence of JOHN CLARKSON, JOHN BAILEY, WILLIAM X [his mark] LONG

At a Court held for Louisa County the 14th day of March 1742.
This Indenture Receipt and Memorandum of Livery and Seizen were proved by the Oaths of JOHN CLARKSON, JOHN BAILEY and WILLIAM LONG the Witnesses thereto and Ordered to be Recorded. Test JAMES LITTLEPAGE, Clk.
Truly recorded by JAS. LITTLE

-Pursuant to an order of Louisa County Cort dated the 14th of feb. 1742. We the subscribers being first sworn did on this day meet JOHN HACKET on a plantation belonging to his father THOMAS HACKET to value the Improvements mad on 1200 acres of Land belonging to the said THOMAS HACKET lying on both sides of the South Branch of the North fork of James River in the aforesaid County where we find as followeth to Wit

To 10 head of Cattel..........30.00.0
To 1 dwelling house..........20.00.0
To 4 Acres of well cleared land..........20.00.0

To 1432 Rales..04.06.0
To 450 Appell Trees..22.10.0
To 130 peach Trees...03.05.0
To 2 Jurneys up to the said plantation & the charges..04.10.0
To 2 Jurneys to Hanover Court......................................01.00.0

p. Louisa County Deed Book A 14th March 1742

63 To moving CHARLES BLACKSTONE and his
household goods to the said plantation.............10.00.0
To 3 bushels & a peek of Corn......................................00.06.6
To 220 pounds of Bacon...05.12.6
To 1 Jurney up with fore negros and provisions............15.00.0
To half a barrel of Corn and carrying it to Mill................00.07.0
To 2 Jurneys to Louisa Court...01.00.0
To Arms and Ammonishon to gard the said plantation..02.10.0
To all the Charges of Entring Surving and Chain
carrers and going to the Secetary's Offis...........22.01.6
To 1 gallon and a half of brandy and 1 lock..................00.15.0
To 3 axis and 2 hose and a set of wegges.....................01.18.6
To a bead...02.00.0
To 1 good pot & hook & frin pann and mortar..............01.15.0
168.17.0

Note that we recev. fore working negros follows on the said plantation which we valued to 200 pounds and five work horses and a mare and colt which we valued to 60 pounds but not being satisfied wheather such negros and horses were allowed as proper improvements to said Land we therefore submit them to as our worships more wiser Opinyons sartified under our hands this 8th day of March 1742. BENJAMIN HENSLEE JOS. MARTIN
At a Court held for Louisa County on Monday the 14th day of March 1742.
This Account of the valuation of the Improvements made on the land of THOMAS HACKET within mentioned being this day returned in Court is ordered to be Recorded; JOHN HACKET son of the said THOMAS having first made oath that the said Improvements have never before been valued to saver any Land that he knows of.

Test JAMES LITTLEPAGE, Clk.
Truly recorded by JAM. LITTLEPAGE, Clk.

p. Louisa County Deed Book A 11th April 1743

64 -The improvements of Mr. HENRY BIBs valed by us the subscribers to teen pounds hous fensen and tow negrous working their valed to seventy five pounds and on young hors at six pounds. valed by us the subscribers
JOHN KENBROW, GEORGE BERY
At a Court held for Louisa County on Monday the 11th day of April 1743.
This account of the Valuation of the Improvements on the Land of HENRY BIBB [pursuant to

an order of the Last Court] being this day returned in Court and Ordered to be Recorded: the said HENRY having first made Oath that the said Improvements have never before been valued to save any Land. Test JAMES LITTLEPAGE, Clk.
Truly Recorded by JAMES LITTLEPAGE, Clk.

-This Indenture made the XI day of April in the year of our Lord MDCCXLI Between JOHN PRICE of the County of Louisa [son of JOHN PRICE, decd. late of Hanover County] of the one part And ISAAC CLARKE of the aforesaid County of Louisa Carpenter of the other part. Witnesseth that the said JOHN PRICE [aged sixteen years the 7 day of January last] by and with the approbation and consent of the Court of the said County of Louisa hath and by these presents doth bind & put himself Apprentice unto the said ISAAC CLARKE, Faithfully and truly to serve him the said ISAAC after the manner of an Apprentice until he shall attain to the full age of XXI years.
In Consideration whereof the said ISAAC CLARKE doth hereby Covenant promise and agree to and with the said JOHN PRICE to use the utmost of his Endeavour to teach and instruct or cause to be taught and instructed the said JOHN in the Trade Art or Mystery of a Carpenter and during the time of his Apprenticeship to find provide and allow him sufficient Diet Lodging

p. <u>Louisa County Deed Book A 11th April 1743</u>
65 and Apparel and at the expiration thereof to give him a Set of Carpenter Tools and pay him five pounds in a Store. In Witness where of the parties to these presents have interchangably set their hands and seals the day and year first above written.

JOHN PRICE [seal] ISAAC CLARK [seal]

At a Court held for Louisa County on Monday the 11th day of April 1743.
This Indenture executed in Court by the parties thereto with the Consent and approbation of the Court and ordered to be Recorded.

Test JAMES LITTLEPAGE, Clerk

-This Indenture made the fifteenth day of April in the year of our Lord one thousand seven hundred and forty three Between JOHN WILLIAMSON of the parish of Saint Paul's in Hanover County of the one part and ROBERT PRIDDEY of the parish of Saint Martin's and County of Hanover aforesaid of the other part. Witnesseth that the said JOHN WILLIAMSON for and in consideration of the sum of fifty pounds current money of Virginia to him in hand paid by the said ROBERT PRIDDEY the Receit where of he doth hereby acknowledge and himself to be fully satisfied contented and paid hath given granted Bargained sold enfeoffed and confirmed and by these presents doth grant bargain sell enfeoff and confirm unto the said ROBERT PRIDDY his heirs and assigns for ever one certain parcel or tract of Land containing by estimation Two hundred acres situate lying and being in the Parish of Saint Martin's in Louisa County and is part of a greater tract granted by pattent to the said JOHN WILLIAMSON and the said two hundred acres of Land is bounded as followeth To wit Beginning

p. Louisa County Deed Book A 13th June 1743

66 at the mouth of a Creek Called WILLIAMSONS Creek and runing up the said Creek according to its water courses to the value of fifty two poles to Several marked Saplins at a Spring and Running Thence south forty two degrees and a half West two hundred and eight poles to two corner White oaks standing by a Branch Thence south forty one Degrees west one hundred sixty nine poles to a corner pine Thence south fifty four Degrees East sixty four poles to a Corner pine Thence North thirty Eight degrees East one hundred Eighty four poles to several marked White oaks in FINNEY's line Thence along FINNEY's Line south fifty four Degrees East one hundred forty four poles to a Corner Black oak and White Oak Thence North sixty degrees East sixty four poles to a White oak standing on the south side of the South Anna River and Runnng thence up the said River the Value of Two hundred Thirty six poles.to the mouth of the Creek where it first began with all houses orchards gardens fences woods waters and advantages whatsoever to the same belonging in any wise appertaining To Have and To Hold the said Two hundred acres of Land and promises or be there more or less within the bounds above mentioned unto the said ROBERT PRIDDEY his heirs and assigns for ever and the said JOHN WILLIAMSON for himself his heirs Executors and administrators Doth by these presents covenant grant and agree too and with the said ROBERT PRIDDEY his heirs Exrs. Admrs. and assigns that the said parcel or Tract of land is free and clear from all other sales Deeds Leases and Incumbrances whatsoever and that it shall and may be Lawfull too and for the said ROBERT PRIDDEY his heirs Exrs. Admrs. or assigns for ever hereafter fully peaceably and quietly to have hold use possess and enjoy and that the said JOHN WILLIAMSON his heirs Exrs. and Admrs. the above sold land and premises with their and every of their appurtenances unto the said ROBERT PRIDDEY his heirs Exrs. admrs. and assigns against him the said

p. Louisa County Deed Book A 13th June 1743

67 JOHN WILLIAMSON his heirs Exrs. and Admrs. and against all other persons whatsoever Doth by these presents Warrant and for ever will Defend in Witness whereof he hath hereunto sett his hand and seal the day and year first above written.

Signed sealed and Delivered
in presence of us JOHN WILLIAMSON [seal]

WM. STREET, JOHN MICHIE, GEORGE HENDERSON

Memorandum That on the fifteenth day of April in the year of our Lord one thousand seven hundred and forty three peaceable possession and seizen of all the Lands and premises within granted was Delivered by the said JOHN WILLIAMSON unto the said ROBERT PRIDDEY by Turft and Twigg.

In presence of us [blank] JOHN WILLIAMSON

April the 15th 1743 Then Recovered of Mr. ROBERT PRIDDEY the within mentioned consideration of fifty pounds Current money of Virginia in full satisfaction for the within mentioned Tract of Land I say Received by me. JOHN WILLIAMSON

At a Court held for Louisa County on Monday the 13th day of June 1743.

This Indenture Receipt and Memorandum of Livery and Seisen were acknowledged by JOHN WILLIAMSON one of the parties Also PRUDENCE the wife of the said JOHN [being first privily examined] relinquished all her right and title of Dower of in & unto the Lands and appurtenances therein mentioned and ordered to be recorded.

Test JAMES LITTLEPAGE, Clk.

p. <u>Louisa County Deed Book A 13th June 1743</u>

68 -This Indenture made the ninth day of May in the year of our Lord one thousand seven hundred & forty three Between WILLIAM MONKUS of Louisa County of the one part and WILLIAM HENDRICK of Hanover County of the other part. Witnesseth that the said WILLIAM MONKUS for and in consideration of Twenty pounds current money of Virginia in hand paid before the ensealing of these presents to him already paid the receipt whereof he doth hereby confess & acknowledge and himself therewith fuly contented satisfyed and paid & from Every part and parcel thereof the said WILLIAM HENDRICK his heirs Executors and Administrators doth hereby fully clearly and Absolutely Acquit & Discharge Hath Letten aliened Bargained and sold made over and Confirmed & by these presents doth fully clearly and Absolutely lett alien bargain sell make over and confirm unto the said WILLIAM HENDRICK his heirs Executors Admrs. & assigns one Certain Tract or parcell of Land containing four hundred acres situate lying and being in the County of Louisa and bounded as followeth [to wit] Beginning at CHARLES SMITH's Corner Pine & Hicory Saplin runing thence North seventh seven Degrees East two hundred and thirty poles to a Chesnutt and hicory saplins in CHRISTOPHER SMITH's Line and thence along his lines North one hundred and twenty poles to a Red oak Bush thence South Eighty Degrees East sixty two poles to his and Mr. JOHN POINDEXTER's Corner red oak by the side of a Vally thence along POINDEXTER's line North six degrees East one hundred and forty six poles to his corner Several Markt trees in BENJAMIN BROWN's line thence along the same South fifty Eight Degrees west one hundred and thirty four poles to his and AMBROSE JOSHUA SMITH's Corner black oak saplin thence along SMITHS's lines south fifty eight Degrees West one hundred & Eighteen poles to a pine saplin standing on

p. <u>Louisa County Deed Book A 13th June 1743</u>

69 the side of a Hill thence North Eighty two Degrees West at ten poles South fork of Contrary in all one hundred and thirty six poles to a Line South thirty nine Degrees west one hundred and forty five poles to SMITH's Corner several pines in AMBROSE JOSHUA SMITH's line and thence along CHARLES SMITH's line South sixty degrees East one hundred and Eight poles to the Beginning To Have and To Hold and peaceably to enjoy the aforesaid four hundred acres of Land from the claime rite or title of him the said WILLIAM MUNKUS his heirs Exrs. or any other person or persons whatsoever, to the only proper use and behoof of him the said WILLIAM HENDRICK his heirs or assigns forever with all Houses orchards gardens woods ways and underwoods Meadows and Lowground with all of the appurtenances and Improvements thereto belonging & the said WILLIAM MUNKUS for himself his heirs Executors Admrs. &c. doth promise covenant and agree that they will from

time to time and at all times forever hereafter against all and all Manner of persons Whatsoever the rite of the same land Warrant and Defend and the same make good and Mentain to the said WILLIAM HENDRICK his heirs Exrs. or assigns for ever. In Witness hereof the said WILLIAM MONKUS hath hereunto fixed his hand and seal the day and year above written. Signed Sealed and Delivered

In presents of us WILLIAM W [his mark] MONKUS [seal]

THOS. PRESTWOOD, JUN., ANNE O [her mark] WHITE, WM. WHITE

Memorandum That full and Peaceable Possession and Seizen was this day given and Delivered of the land and premises within mentioned by the within named WILLIAM MONKUS to WILLIAM HENDRICK in presents whose names are Subscribed In Witness whereof the said MONKUS hath hereunto fixed his hand and seal this Ninth day of May 1743. WM. W [his mark] MONKUS [seal]

Test ANNE O [her mark] WHITE, WM. WHITE, THOS. PRESTWOOD, JUN.

At a Court held for Louisa County on Monday the 13th June 1743.

This Indenture and Memorandum of Livery of Seisen were acknowledged by WILLIAM MONKUS one of the parties and ordered to be recorded.

Test JAMES LITTLEPAGE, Clk.

p. <u>Louisa County Deed Book A 13th June 1743</u>

70 -This Indenture made the twelvth day of June in the year of our Lord one thousand seven hundred and forty three Between JAMES MERIDETH planter of the one part and JOHN GOODALL planter of the other part. Witnesseth that the said JAMES MERIDETH for and in consideration of fifteen pounds current money of Virginia to him in hand paid by the said JOHN GOODALL at and before the Ensealing and Delivery of these presents, the Receipt Whereof the said JAMES MERIDETH doth hereby confess and acknowledge hath given, granted, Bargained Sold Aliened released and confirmed and by these presents Doth give grant bargain sell alien release and confirm unto the said JOHN GOODALL all that his piece or parcel of land situate lying and being in the County of Louisa and Fredricevile parish Between the two Ridges of Mountain containing by estimation four hundred acres be the same more or less granted to the said JAMES MERIDETH by Patent bearing date the Fifteenth day of October one thousand seven hundred and forty one and bounded as Followeth to wit Beginning at JOSEPH KEATON's corner pine sapling runing thence along his line North one hundred and thirty poles to a hickory in the said line Thence South Eighty five degrees West at sixty Eight a branch at one hundred and twenty four, the North fork of Rocky Creek in all one hundred and forty eight poles to a Red oak and white oak saplings thence South twenty seven degrees West at Ninety three a branch in all one hundred and Ninety eight poles to a pine in the fork of a small Branch thence south fifty five degrees East one hundred and sixty poles to a Red oak on the side of a Hill thence North seventy three degrees East two hundred and forty poles crossing a Branch and the North fork of Rocky Creek to a stake between four pines thence North one hundred and forty four poles to a stake by a Shrubby white oak in JOSEPH KEATON's line and thence along the same South sixty four degrees West one hundred and thirty seven poles to the Beginning together with

all the Improvements whatsoever and also all woods underwoods waies waters and water coursey's and all other profits commodities and advantages To Have and To Hold the said plantation Land and all and singular other the premises with their and every of their appurtenances unto

p. Louisa County Deed Book A 13th June 1743
71 the said JOHN GOODALL his heirs and assigns forever and the said JAMES MERIDETH for himself his heirs Executors and Administrators doth Covenant grant and agree to and with the said JOHN GOODALL his heirs Executors Administrators and assigns in Manner and form Following [that is to say] that the said JAMES MERIDETH at the time of the Ensealing and Delivery hereof is and stands Lawfully Seized of an Absolute and Indefeasable Estate of Inheritance in fee simple of and in the land and other the premises herein Conveyed and every part and parcel thereof and hath good right Title and Lawfull Authority to Grant Bargain and sell the same in Manner aforesaid and that the said JOHN GOODALL his heirs and assigns shall and may from time to time and at all times hereafter quietly and peaceably have hold possess and Enjoy the above Granted land and premises and every part and parcel thereof with the appurtenances without any lawful let suit Trouble Eviction or Molestation of him the said JAMES MERIDETH his heirs or assigns or any other person or persons whatsoever Claiming or to claim by from or under him them or any of them and that free and clear and freely and clearly acquitted and Discharged or by the said JAMES MERIDETH his heirs Executors Administrators or some of any of them from time to time and at all times hereafter kept harmless and Indemnified of and from all and all Manner of former and other bargaines sailes gifts Grants and Intails Dowers and Titles of Dower and all other charge and Incumbrance whatsoever had made comited done or suffered to be had made comited and one by him the said JAMES MERIDETH or by any other person or persons Claiming or to claim by from or under and lastly the said JAMES MERIDETH his heirs Executors and Administrators the said land and Premises herein before Bargained and sold with their and every of their appurtenances unto the said JOHN GOODALL his heirs and assigns will warrent and ever Defend by these presents in Witness whereof the parties to these presents his hand and seal have set the day of the year above written.

Signed Sealed and Delivered in the presence of
DAVID MILLS, WILLIAM BUNCH JAMES X [his mark] MERIDETH [seal]
Received the twelveth day of June one thousand seven hundred and forty three the sum of Fifteen pounds current money of Virginia it being the consideration

p. Louisa County Deed Book A 13th June 1743
72 money within mentioned I say Received of JOHN GOODALL & me.
Test DAVID MILLS, WILLIAM BUNCH JAMES X [his mark] MERIDETH
Memorandum The Quiet and peaceable possession of the within granted land and premises was given by the within JAMES MERIDETH unto the within JOHN GOODALL by Delivery of Turf and Twig of the same as the usual Symboles of Livery and Seizen as Witness

my hand this Twelveth day of June 1743.

Testes DAVID MILLS, WILLIAM BUNCH JAMES X [his mark] MERIDETH

At a Court held for Louisa County on Monday the XIII day of June 1743.
This Indenture Receipt and Memorandum of Livery of Seisen were acknowledged by JAMES MERIDETH one of the Parties, also LUCRETIA the wife of the said JAMES [being first privily examined] Relinquishes all her Right and Title of Dower of in and unto the Lands and appurtenances, therein mentioned and ordered to be recorded.

Test JAMES LITTLEPAGE, Clk.

-This Indenture made this first day of June in the year of our Lord God one thousand seven hundred and forty three Between RICHARD BLALACK of Louisa County of the one part and PHILIP TIMBERLAKE of the aforesaid County of the other part. Witnesseth that the said RICHARD BLALACK for and in consideration of the sum of thirty pounds Sterling to him in hand paid by the said PHILIP TIMBERLAKE before the sealing and Delivery of these presents the Receipt whereof he the said RICHARD BLALACK doth hereby acknowledge and thereof doth clearly acquit and discharge the said PHILIP TIMBERLAKE his heirs and assigns by these presents Hath

p. Louisa County Deed Book A 13th June 1743

73 Granted Bargained Sold Enfeoff and Confirmed and by these presents doth Grant Bargain Sell enfeoff and Confirm unto the said PHILIP TIMBERLAKE one certain Tract or parcel of Land containing one hundred and four acres of Land situate lying and being in the County aforesaid and on the lower side of Cubb Creek Bounded as followeth Beginning at WILLIAM BLALACK's corner Maple standing on the lower side of Cubb Creek near the crossing place of the Road thence South sixty eight East on WILLIAM BLALACK's line one hundred poles to his Schrubby white oak saplin being a corner of the said WILLIAM thence South fifty five East one hundred and seven poles to a corner of several trees standing by the Roadside being another Corner of the said WILLIAM's, thence South thirty two west one hundred and fifty poles to RICHARD HARRIS's corner Schrubby white oak and Pine, Thence on HARRIS's line, North fifty two west one hundred eighty eight poles to Cubb Creek thence up the same following the water courses to the beginning to have and to hold the one hundred and four acres of land according to the above bounds be the same more or less to the said PHILIP TIMBERLAKE his heirs and assigns for ever Together with the Houses and appurtenances thereunto belonging and appertaining to the said PHILIP TIMBERLAKE his heirs and assigns forever to the only proper use and behoof of him the said PHILIP TIMBERLAKE his heirs and assigns forever more free and clear from all or any claime Title or Demand of him the said RICHARD BLALACK his heirs and of all or any other person or persons whatsoever Claiming by from or under him them or any of them and the said RICHARD BLALACK for himself his heirs &c. doth hereby Covenant promise and agree to and with the said TIMBERLAKE his heirs &c. that he the said RICHARD BLALACK shall and will at any time or times hereafter when thereunto Required by the said TIMBERLAKE or his heirs make such further and other Conveyance for the better Transforming and assessing the said

Land unto the said PHILIP TIMBERLAKE his heirs and assigns in Such manner and by such Deed as he the said TIMBERLAKE his heirs and assigns they or any of them shall at any Time hereafter at the Cost of the said TIMBERLAKE his heirs &c. Require and also that he the said RICHARD BLALACK his heirs &c. all the promise aforesaid with the appurtenances will warrant and forever by these presents unto the said PHILIP TIMBERLAKE his heirs

p. Louisa County Deed Book A 13th June 1743

74 and assigns against him the said RICHARD BLALACK his heirs and against all and Every other person or persons Whatsoever In Witness whereof the said RICHARD BLALACK hath hereunto set his hand and seal the day and year first above written.

Sealed and Delivered in presence of us

ROGER THOMPSON, HUMPHRY [HP} PARISH, JEREMIAH GLEN RICHARD BLALACK [seal]

Memorandum That on this [blank] day of one thousand seven hundred and forty three I RICHARD BLALACK do acknowledge to have made Livery of Seizen of the land and premises in the within Deed contained by the Delivery of Turf and Twigg of the said land unto the said PHILIP TIMBERLAKE his heirs & assigns forever according to the form and effect of the Within Deed. Witness my hand and seal the day and year within Written.

Signed Sealed and Delivered

ROGER THOMPSON, HUMPHRY [HP} PARISH, JEREMIAH GLEN RICHARD BLALACK [seal]

At a Court held for Louisa County on Monday the 13th June 1743.

This Indenture and Memorandum of Livery of Seisin were acknowledged by RICHARD BLALACK one of the parties, also RACHEL the wife of the said RICHARD [being first privily examined] Relinquished all her Rights Title of Dower of in and unto the Lands and appurtenances therein mentioned and ordered to be Recorded.

Test JAMES LITTLEPAGE, Clk.

p. Louisa County Deed Book A 13th June 1743

75 -This Indenture made this thirteenth day of June in the sixteenth year of the Reign of our Sovereign Lord George the Second by the Grace of God of Great Britain France and Ireland King Defender of the Faith &c. and in the year of our Lord Christ one thousand seven hundred and fourty three Between RICHARD BROOKS of the Parish of Fredricksville and County of Louisa Planter of the one part and DAVID GENTRY and SARAH GENTRY wife to the said DAVID GENTRY of the same Parish and County of the other part. Witnesseth, that I the said RICHARD BROOKS out of paturnal affection which I have and do bear to my said son in Law DAVID GENTRY and my Daughter above named, and for divers other causes thereto me moving, have given, granted, donated and forever made over and by these presents, for the above consideration, do fully and absolutely grant donate, and forever make over enfeoff and Confirm unto the said DAVID GENTRY and SARAH GENTRY, and their Heirs, all that Dividend Tract or parcel of land situate lying and being on Dirty Swamp in the Parish of Fredricksville, and County of Louisa containing by estimation one Hundred acres be the same more or less and Bounded as followeth Beginning at a Shrubby White oak runing thence South twenty three Degrees west one hundred Poles to Pointer's thence North sixty

seven Degrees west one hundred and sixty poles to Pointer's, thence North twenty three Degrees east one Hundred poles to Pointer's, thence south sixty seven Degrees East one hundred and sixty poles to the first Station Together with all woods underwoods, ways, waters and water courses, Feedings Pastures, Easements, Commodities Hereditaments and Appurtenances whatsoever to the same belonging or in any wise appertaining and the Reversion and Reversions Remainder and Remainders and all and singular the Estate, Right title Property Claime and Demand of me the said RICHARD BROOKS of in or to the premises or any part thereof with the appurtenances To Have and To Hold the said Dividend Tract or parcel of Land, and all and singular other the premises hereby given granted, donated and made over with their and every of their appurtenances unto the said DAVID GENTRY and SARAH GENTRY their heirs and assigns, to the only proper use and behoof of them the said DAVID GENTRY and SARAH GENTRY their heirs and assigns for

p. <u>Louisa County Deed Book A 13th June 1743</u>

76 ever and I the said RICHARD BROOKS for myself and my heirs the said Tract or Parcel of Land and Premises with the appurtenances unto the said DAVID GENTRY and SARAH GENTRY and their heirs against me the said RICHARD BROOKS, my heirs and assigns and all and every other person or persons whatsoever Lawfully Claiming or to Claim by from or under me, them or any of them shall and will warrant and forever defend by these presents. In Witness whereof I the said RICHARD BROOKS have hereunto set my hand and seal the date above mentioned.

Sealed and Delivered in presence of
JOHN VENABLE, JOHN CLARK RICHARD R [his mark] BROOKS [seal]

Memorandum That Livery and Seisen of the lands and appurtenances within mentioned was given to the within named DAVID GENTRY and SARAH GENTRY by the within named RICHARD BROOKS this 13th day of June on thousand seven hundred and forty three.

Sealed and Delivered in presence of
JOHN VENABLE, JOHN CLARK RICHARD R [his mark] BROOKS [seal]

At a Court for Louisa County on Monday the 13th June 1743.
This Indenture and Memorandum of Livery and Seisen were acknowledged by RICHARD BROOKS one of the parties, and ordered to be Recorded. Test JAMES LITTLEPAGE, Clk.

p. <u>Louisa County Deed Book A 13th June 1743</u>

77 -This Indenture made the thirteenth day of June in the sixteenth year of the Reign of our Sovereign Lord George the Second by the Grace of God of Great Brittain, France and Ireland King Defender of the Faith &c. and in the year of our Lord Christ one thousand seven hundred and fourty three. Between RICHARD BROOKS of the parish of Fredericksville and County of Louisa Planter, of the one part and NICHOLAS GENTRY the younger, and MARY GENTRY wife to the said NICHOLAS GENTRY of the same parish and County of the other part. Witnesseth, that I the said RICHARD BROOKS, out of the Paturnal affection which I have and do bear to my said son in Law NICHOLAS GENTRY and To my Daughter MARY GENTRY above named, and for divers other causes thereto me moving, have given, granted,

donated and forever made over and by these presents, for the above consideration, do fully and absolutely give, grant, donate, and forever make over Enfeoff and Confirm unto the said NICHOLAS GENTRY and MARY GENTRY, and their Heirs, all that Dividend Tract or parcel of land situate lying and being on Dirty Swamp in the Parish of Fredricksville, and County of Louisa containing by estimation one Hundred acres be the same more or less and Bounded thus [viz.] Beginning at a Corner Three Shruby white oaks, Runing thence South, twenty three degrees west one hundred poles to a shruby white oak, thence North sixty seven degrees West one hundred sixty poles to Pointer's, thence North twenty three degrees East one hundred poles to several marked Trees, Thence South sixty seven degreed East one hundred and sixty poles to the first station, Together with all woods, underwoods, ways, waters and water courses, Feedings, Pastures Easements, Commodities, Hereditaments, and appurtenances, and the Reversion and Reversions, Remainder and Remainders, and all and singular, the Estate, Right, Title, Property claime and Demand of me the said RICHARD BROOKS, of in, or to the premises or any part thereof, with the appurtenances, To Have and

p. Louisa County Deed Book A 13th June 1743

78 to hold the said Dividend Tract or Parcel of land and all and singular other the premises hereby Given, Granted, Donate and made over, with their and Every of their appurtenances unto the said NICHOLAS GENTRY and MARY GENTRY their heirs and assigns, to the only proper use and behoof of them the said NICHOLAS GENTRY and MARY GENTRY, their heirs and assigns forever and I the said RICHARD BROOKS for myself and my heirs the said Tract or Parcel of Land and Premises with the appurtenances unto the said NICHOLAS GENTRY and MARY GENTRY and their heirs against me the said RICHARD BROOKS, my heirs and assigns and all and every other person or persons whatsoever Lawfully Claiming or to Claim by from or under me, them or any of them shall and will warrant and forever defend by these presents. In Witness whereof I the said RICHARD BROOKS have hereunto set my hand and seal the date above mentioned.

Sealed and Delivered in presence of

JOHN VENABLE, JOHN CLARK RICHARD R [his mark] BROOKS [seal]

Memorandum that Livery and Seisen of the lands and appurtenances within mentioned was given to the within named NICHOLAS GENTRY and MARY GENTRY by the within named RICHARD BROOKS this 13th day of June on thousand seven hundred and forty three.

Sealed and Delivered in presence of

JOHN VENABLE, JOHN CLARK RICHARD R [his mark] BROOKS [seal]

At a Court for Louisa County on Monday the 13th June 1743.

This Indenture and Memorandum of Livery and Seisen were acknowledged by RICHARD BROOKS one of the parties, and ordered to be Recorded. Test JAMES LITTLEPAGE, Clk.

p. Louisa County Deed Book A 13th June 1743

79 -This Indenture made this thirteenth day of June in the year of our Lord Christ one thousand seven hundred and forty three between HARDING BURNLEY of the Parish of Saint Paul in the County of Hanover of the one part, and WILLIAM BIBB of the parish of

Saint Martin in the County aforesaid of the other part. Witnesseth that the said HARDING BURNLEY for and in consideration of the sum of Thirty pounds current money to him in hand paid before the sealing and Delivery of these presents the receipt whereof he doth hereby acknowledge and himself fully satisfied contented and paid, and thereof and every part and parcel thereof doth hereby acquit and discharge the said WILLIAM BIBB his heirs Executors, Administrators &c. forever Hath Granted Sold aliened enfeoffed and Confirmed and these presents doth grant sell alien enfeoff and confirm unto the said WILLIAM BIBB his heirs and assigns for ever one certain tract or parcel of Land situate lying and being in the Parish of Fredricksville and County of Louisa containing by Estimation three hundred acres be the same more or less bounded as followeth [to wit] beginning at a Corner pine in the line of SAMUEL THOMSON runing thence North sixty four degrees West Dividing this land from the land of JAMES ROACH two hundred Ninety two poles to a Poplar in BURNLEY's line by the side of a Branch, thence North seven Degrees west forty six poles to two Blazed Pines thence North seventy eight degrees East twenty six poles to a Hickory Grub in the midst of several Pointer's in CHAMPNESS TERRY's Line thence Dividing this land from the land of the said TERRY's South Eleven degrees west twenty nine poles for Red oak saplin thence south twenty two degrees east fourteen poles to a pine in SAMUEL THOMPSON's line, thence on his line south eighty four degrees West Eighty three poles to the Beginning To Have and To Hold and peaceably to enjoy the aforesaid three hundred acres of land above bounded with all Houses orchards, gardens, woods, ways waters and under woods and Meadow Grounds with all other and singular the Improvements and appurtenances thereunto belonging or in any wise appertaining from

p. <u>Louisa County Deed Book A 13th June 1743</u>

80 the claime, Right or Title of him the said HARDING BURNLEY his heirs, Executors &c. or any other person or persons Whatsoever to the only proper use and behoof of him the said WILLIAM BIBB his heirs Executors or assigns for ever and the said HARDING BURNLEY for himself his heirs, Executors &c. doth covenant promise and agree that he will from time to time and at all times Hereafter against all persons Whatsoever the Right of the above said land and premises warrant and forever Defend to the said WILLIAM BIBB his heirs or assigns and the said BURNELY doth for Himself his heirs &c. further promise that he shall and will be ready at all times forever hereafter to make any further Right Conveyance or Title that he the said WILLIAM BIBB his heirs or assigns or his or their Council learned in the Law shall lawfully required. In Witness whereof the said HARDING BURNLEY hath hereunto set his hand and fixed his seal the day and year first above written.

Signed Sealed & Delivered in presence of us HARD. BURNLEY [seal]

BENJA. HANSON, JAMES GOODALL, CHAMPNESS TERRY

Memorandum that on the day and year first within written peaceable and quiet possession of the land and premises within Granted and sold was had and taken by the within Named HARDING BURNLEY and by him Delivered over unto the within named WILLIAM BIBB to hold to him his Heirs and assigns forever according to the purport true Intent and Meaning of the within mentioned Indenture.

In presence of us HARD. BURNLEY [seal]
BENJA. HANSON, JAMES GOODALL, CHAMPNESS TERRY

p. Louisa County Deed Book A 13th June 1743
81 At a Court held for Louisa County on Monday the 13th June 1743.
This Indenture and Memorandum of Livery of Seisen were acknowledged by HARDEN BURNLEY one of the parties and ordered to be Recorded.

Test JAMES LITTLEPAGE, Clk.
Truly recorded by JAS. LITTLEPAGE, Clk.

-This Indenture made the thirteenth day of June in the year of our Lord Christ one thousand seven hundred and forty three, Between HARDEN BURNLEY of the parish of Saint Paul in the County of Hanover of the one part and JAMES ROACH of the parish of Fredricksville in the County of Louisa of the other part. Witnesseth that the said HARDEN BURNLEY for and in consideration of the sum of twenty pounds current money of Virginia to him in hand paid by the said JAMES ROACH at and before the Ensealing and Delivery of these presents the Receipt Whereof he doth hereby acknowledge, and thereof and of every part and parcel of the same doth clearly acquit and Discharge the said JAMES ROACH his Executors and Administrators and every of them by these presents for the consideration above set down doth Grant alien, Release Enfeoffe and Perpetually confirm unto the said JAMES ROACH and to his heirs and assigns forever all that the said HARDEN BURNLEY his parcel or tract of land containing two hundred acres as the same is already laid of lying in the fork of Golden Mine Creek in the aforesaid Parish of Fredricksville and County of Louisa. Beginning at a pine Commonly known by the name of BRACKS pine and is Bounded on two sides by the lines of Capt. JOHN BICKERTON's and on the other two sides, by the land of the said BURNLEY being the moiety of use property and claim of him the said HARDEN BURNLEY his heirs or assigns of in or unto the premises and the Reversion and Reversions Remainder and Remainders Yearly and other Rents and Profits of the

p. Louisa County Deed Book A 13th June 1743
82 premises and of every part and parcell thereof to have and to hold the said two hundred acres of land and all and singular other the premises herein before mentioned and Intended to be hereby granted with their and every of their appurtenances unto the said JAMES ROACH and his heirs to the only use of the said JAMES ROACH and of his Heirs and assigns for ever, and the said HARDEN BURNLEY for himself his heirs Executors and Administrators doth covenant and grant to and with the said JAMES ROACH his heirs and assigns by these presents that he the said HARDEN BURNLEY now is and standeth lawfully and Rightfully seised of and in the said two hundred acres of land above bounded and premises of a good sure perfect absolute and Indefeasable Estate in fee simple and now hath good Right full power and Lawful and absolute authority to grant and convey the same according to the purport true Intent and Meaning of these presents and that it shall and may be Lawfull to and for the said JAMES ROACH his heirs and assigns from

time to time and at all times forever hereafter peaceably and quietly to have hold occupy possess use and enjoy the said two hundred acres of land above bounded and all and singular other the premises Herein before mentioned and Intended to be hereby Granted with their appurtenances without any Lawfull let suit Trouble or Interruption of him the said HARDEN BURNLEY his heirs or assigns or any other person or persons whatsoever Discharge of and from all Incumbrances of Evictions whatsoever the Quit Rents from hence forth to grow due and payable to our Sovereign Lord the King his heirs and Successors only Excepted and foreprized and the said BURNLEY for himself his heirs Executors and Administrators the aforesaid Granted premises with their appurtenances unto the said JAMES ROACH and his Heirs against him the said HARDEN BURNLEY and his heirs

p. Louisa County Deed Book A 13th June 1743
83 and all Claiming or to Claim Right to from or under him them or any of them or any other person or persons whatsoever have and will warrant and forever defend by these presents. In Witness whereof the said HARDEN BURNLEY to these presents Interchangeably hath set his hand and affixed his seal the day and year first above Written.
Sign'd Sealed & Delivered In the presence of
JAMES GOODALL, CHAMPNESS TERRY, BENJA. HENSON HARD. BURNLEY [seal]
Received of JAMES ROACH the sum of Twenty pounds current money being the consideration within mentioned Witness my hand this thirteenth day of June Anno Domini, one thousand seven hundred and forty three. HARD. BURNLEY
Memorandum That peaceable and Quiet possession of the within mentioned premises was first had and taken by the within named HARDEN BURNLEY and by him given to the within Named JAMES ROACH by the Delivery of Turf and Twigg of the Ground of the said Land as the usual Symbolls of Livery of Seisen to be by him held according to the within written Indenture. In Witness whereof the said HARDEN BURNLEY hath hereunto set his hand and seal this 13th day of June Anno Domini MDCCXXXIII. HARD. BURNLEY [seal]
Test JAMES GOODALL, CHAMPNESS TERRY, BENJA. HENSON
At a Court held for Louisa County on Monday the 13th day June 1743.
This Indenture Receipt and Memorandum of Livery of Seisen were acknowledged by HARDEN BURNLEY one of the Parties and were ordered to be recorded.
Test JAMES LITTLEPAGE, Clk. Truly recorded by JAS. LITTLEPAGE, Clk.

p. Louisa County Deed Book A 13th June 1743
84 -This Indenture made this thirteenth day of June in the year of our Lord Christ one thousand seven hundred and forty three Between HARDING BURNLEY of the parish of St. Paul in the County of Louisa of the one part and CHAMPNESS TERRY of the parish of Fredricksville and County of Louisa of the other part. Witnesseth that the said HARDING BURNLEY for and in consideration of the sum of twelve pounds current money to him in hand paid before the sealing and delivery of these presents the receipt whereof he doth hereby acknowledge and himself therewith fully satisfied and paid and thereof and every part and parcel thereof doth hereby acquit and discharge the said CHAMPNESS TERRY his

heirs Executors Administrators &c. for ever hath granted sold aliened enfeoffed and confirmed and by these presents doth grant sell alien enfeoff and confirm unto the said CHAMPNESS TERRY his heirs and assigns for ever a certain tract or parcel of land situate lying and being in the parish of Fredericksville and County of Louisa containing by estimation three hundred acres be the same more or less [which is part of a tract of land granted to the said HARDING BURNLEY by pat. bearing date the twenty first day of November one thousand seven hundred and thirty four] and is bounded as followeth [to wit] Beginning at the said BURNLEY's corner three pines in the line of Col. JOHN SYME running thence south thirty five degrees north three hundred twenty six poles to the said BURNLEY's corner pine in the said line thence on the said BURNLEY's north twenty two degrees west fourteen poles to a corner red oake saplin thence north seven degrees east twenty poles to his corner red oak thence north nine degrees west one hundred and eighty poles to a corner hickory grub in the midst of several pinefors in CHAMPNESS TERRY's line thence north seventy six degrees East three hundred and thirty four poles to SYME's three pines thence along his line fourty eight degrees East one hundred fifteen poles to the beginning To have and to hold peaceably and enjoy the aforesaid three hundred acres of land above bounded with all houses orchards gardens woods ways waters underwoods and meadow grounds with all other and singular the improvements and appurtenances thereunto containing or in any wise appertaining of him the said HARDING BURNLEY his heirs Executors or any other person or persons whatsoever for the only proper use and behoof of him the said CHAMPNESS TERRY his heirs Executors or assigns forever and the said HARDING BURNLEY for himself his heirs and Executors &c. doth covenant promise and agree that he will from time to time and at all times hereafter against all persons whatsoever the right of the above said land and premises warrant and forever defend to the said CHAMPNESS TERRY his heirs and assigns and the said BURNLEY doth for himself his heirs &c. further promise that he shall and will be ready at all times hereafter to make any further right convey Council learned in the Law shall lawfully require In Witness whereof the said HARDING BURNLEY hath hereunto set his hand and fixed his seal the day and year first above written.

Signed Sealed & delivered in presence of us
JAS. GOODALL, BENJAM. HENSON, PHILIP TIMBERLAKE HARD. BURNLEY [seal]

p. <u>Louisa County Deed Book A 13th June 1743</u>
85 Memorandum that on the day and year first written peaceable and quiet possession of the said land and premises within named was sold by the within named HARDING BURNLEY and by him delivered over unto the within named CHAMPNESS TERRY to hold to him his heirs and assigns forever according the purport his intent and meaning of the within mentioned Indenture.

Signed Sealed & delivered in presence of us
JAS. GOODALL, BENJAM. HENSON, PHILIP TIMBERLAKE HARD. BURNLEY [seal]
At a Court held for Louisa County on Monday the 13th June 1743. Anno 1743.
This Indenture and Memorandum of Livery of Siesen were acknowledged by HARDING BURNLEY one of the parties and were ordered to be recorded.

Test JAMES LITTLEPAGE, Clk.
Test JAS. LITTLEPAGE, Clerk

-This Indenture made the thirteenth day of June in the year of our Lord Christ one thousand seven hundred and forty three Between WILLIAM STAPLES of Saint Paul's Parish in the County of Hanover planter of the one part and RICHARD BRIGGS of St. Martins parish in the county of Louisa planter of the other part. Witnesseth that the said STAPLES for and in consideration of the sum of two thousand pounds of Lawfull Tobacco to him in hand paid by the said RICHARD BRIGGS the receipt endorsed whereof he the said STAPLES acknowledged thereof and every part thereof doth clearly acquit discharge the said RICHARD BRIGGS his heirs Executors Administrators forever by these profits hath given granted bargained or sold aliened & confirmed unto the said BRIGGS his heirs forever all that dividend tract or parcell of land containing one hundred seventy one acres lying & being on both sides the North fork of the South Anna River in the County of Louisa as aforesaid it being part of three hundred & forty five acres granted to the said STAPLES by patent bounded as followeth [to wit] Beginning at several pines corner to JOHN SMITHINGS house north forty six degrees west twenty poles to a pine in Colonel MERIWETHER's line thence with his line south fifty & a half degrees west one hundred forty six poles to a pine thence south thirty seven degrees & a half west one hundred thirty nine poles to a pine, thence south eighty eight degrees & a half east one hundred ninety six poles to a stake & three pines on a hill side in JOHN SMITHING's line thence with his line north six degrees east to the beginning with all woods underwoods ways waters & water courses gardens pastures easements commodities hereditaments & appurtenances whatsoever to the same belonging or in any wise appertaining to the reversion reversions remainder and remainders & all and singular the estate right title property claims & demand of the said STAPLES of in or to the premises or any part thereof with the appurtenances To Have and To Hold the said dividend tract or parcel of land and all & singular other with the premises & their and every of their appurtenances unto the said BRIGGS & his heirs to the only proper use and behoof of him the said BRIGGS forever unto the said STAPLES for himself & his heirs the said tract or parcel of land & premises with the appurtenances unto the said BRIGGS & his heirs against him the said STAPLES all & every other person or persons Lawfully claim or claiming by from or under him them or any of them shall & will warrant forever defend by these presents. In Witness whereof he the said WILLIAM STAPLES hath hereunto set his hand and affixed his seal the day of the date of these presents above mentioned.

Signed & Delivered in the presence of
JOHN STAPLES, WILLIAM LONG WILLIAM STAPLES [seal]

p. <u>Louisa County Deed Book A 13th June 1743</u>
86 June 13th 1743 Received of RICHARD BRIGGS two thousand pounds of Lawfull Tobacco it being in full for the Lands and premises within mentioned I say received.
JOHN STAPLES, WILLIAM LONG WILLIAM STAPLES [seal]

Memorandum that on the thirteenth day of June 1743. This day a quiet and peaceable possession of the Land tenements & hereditaments within mentioned was had and taken by the within named RICHARD BRIGGS to the use of him his heirs or forever according to the form of the within written deed.

In the presence of us

JOHN STAPLES, WILLIAM LONG WILLIAM STAPLES [seal]

At a Court held for Louisa County on Monday the 13th day of June 1743. This Indenture receipt and Memorandum of Livery of Seisen were acknowledged by WILLIAM STAPLES one of the parties and were ordered to be recorded.

Test JAMES LITTLEPAGE, Clk. Truly recorded

-This Indenture made this eleventh day of July in the year of our Lord Christ one thousand seven hundred and forty three Between DAVID WATTS of Fredricksville Parish in Louisa County of the one part and ROBERT ROWE of the aforesaid parish & County of the other part. Witnesseth that the said DAVID WATTS for and in consideration of the sum of thirty pounds current money of Virginia to him in hand paid by the said ROBERT ROWE at and before the ensealing and delivery of these presents the receipt thereof he doth hereby acknowledge and thereof and of every part and parcell of the same doth hereby acquit and discharge the said ROBERT ROWE his Executors and Administrators and every of them by these presents for the consideration above do grant, alien, release, enfeoff and perpetually confirm unto the said ROBERT ROWE and to his heirs and assigns forever all that the said DAVID WATTS his parcell & tract of land containing three hundred acres lying and being in the parish and County aforesaid at the main fork of Pritties Creek and is bounded as followeth [to wit] beginning at AMBROSE JOSHUA SMITH's corner two shruby white oaks and runing thence along his line for thirty three degrees west at fifty six pole south fork of Pritties Creek in all eighty four poles to two pines in SMITH's line thence south seventy four degrees east sixty poles to a spanish oak on the edge of a Branch thence north seventy seven degrees east forty six poles to a pine thence north twenty four degrees east at twenty the south fork of Pritties Creek in all eighty two poles to a white oak and a pine in GOOCH's and HICKMAN's line, thence along their line north fifty degrees west at one hundred Middle fork at two hundred fifty two

p. <u>Louisa County Deed Book A 11th July 1743</u>

87 main fork of Pritties Creek in all three hundred and seventy two poles to a Gum and pine by a small branch in the said line thence south forty degrees west, one hundred and fifty two poles to a stake between a white oak saplin and a pine thence south forty one degrees east one hundred and fifteen poles to several pines in AMBROSE JOSHUA SMITH's line, thence along his lines north fifty four degrees east at one hundred and fifteen the main fork of Pritties Creek in all one hundred & fifty four poles to a stake by a meadow and a great pine marked AIS and thence south forty four degrees east of ninety south the middle fork in all one hundred and twenty four poles beginning which said three hundred acres of Land above Bounded to the said DAVID WATTS by patent and bearing date the fifth day of June and the said seven hundred and thirty six and all the said Right Title aforesaid property

and claim of him the said DAVID ROWE his heirs or assigns of in or unto the premises and the reversion and reversions remainder and remainders yearly and other rents and profits of the premises and of every part and parcel thereof To Have and To Hold the said three hundred acres as above bounded and all and singular other the premises herein before mentioned intended to be hereby granted with their and every of their appurtenances unto the said ROBERT ROWE and his heirs to the only use of the said ROBERT ROWE his heirs and assigns forever and the said DAVID WATTS for himself his heirs Executors and Administrators doth covenant and grant to and with the said ROBERT ROWE his heirs and assigns by these presents that he the said DAVID WATTS now is in the said three hundred acres of land above bounded and premises of a good sure perfect absolute and indefeasible estate in fee simple and now hath full power and Lawfull and absolute authority to grant and convey the same according to the purport, his intent and meaning of these presents and that it shall and may be perfect to and for the said ROBERT ROWE his heirs and assigns from time to time and at all times forever hereafter peaceably and quietly to have hold occupy possess now and enjoy the said three hundred acres of Land and all and singular other the premises herein before mentioned and intended to hereby grant with their and every of their appurtenances [line unreadable] his heirs or assigns or any other person or persons whatsoever discharged of the incumbrances whatsoever the Quitrents from henceforth to grow unto our Sovereign Lord the King his heirs and successors only excepted and foreprized and the said DAVID WATTS for himself his heirs Executors Administrators the aforesaid premises with their appurtenances unto the said ROBERT ROWE and his heirs and all claiming and to claim right in by from or under him them or any of them or any other person or persons whatsoever have and will warrant and for ever defend by these presents. In Witness whereof the said DAVID WATTS to these presents hath interchangeably set his hand and affixed his seal the day and year first above written.

in the presence of [blank] DAVID WATTS [seal]

Memorandum that peaceably and quiet possession of the within mentioned premises was first had and acknowledged and taken by the within named DAVID WATTS and by him given to the within named ROBERT ROWE by the delivery of Turf and Twigg of the ground

p. Louisa County Deed Book A 11th July 1743

88 of the said Land as the real Symbolls of Livery of Seisen to be by him held according to the within written Indenture. In Witness whereof the said DAVID WATTS hath hereunto set his hand and seal this eleventh day of July Anno Domini. DAVID WATTS

At a Court held for Louisa County on Monday the XIth day of July 1743.

This Indenture & Memorandum of livery of seisen were this day in open Court acknowledged by DAVID WATTS to be his Act & Deed by the Court admitted to record & is recorded.

Truly Test JAS. LITTLEPAGE, Clk. Recorded

-This Indenture made the eighth day of March in the sixteenth year of the Reign of our Sovereign Lord George the Second by the Grace of God of Great Brittain, France and Ireland King Defender of the Faith &c. and in the year of our Lord Christ one thousand seven hundred and forty two three. Between JOHN THOMPSON, of the County of Hanover Merchant of the one part and ANDREW ROE of the County of Louisa planter of the other part Witnesseth that the said JOHN THOMPSON for and in consideration of the sum of thirty five pounds current money of Virginia to him in hand paid or to be paid at or before the ensealing and delivery of these presents the recd. whereof the said THOMPSON doth hereby acknowledge and himself therewith to be fully contented satisfied and paid and thereof and of every part and parcel thereof doth acquit exonerate and discharge the said ANDREW ROE and his Executors Advisory of them hath given granted bargained sold aliened conveyed and enfeoffed and by these presents for himself his heirs Executors and Administrators doth grant bargain sell alien convey and enfeoff the said THOMPSON's tract or parcel of Land lying and being in the County of Louisa between the two Ledges of Mountains and upon both sides of the south branch of the north fork of the James River containing by estimation five hundred and twenty four acres be the same more or less and bounded as followeth [to wit] beginning at Maj. JOHN HENRY's corner four Black Gums and red oak on the north side the said River runing thence along the said HENRY's line north sixty two poles to a red oak in this line thence east one hundred and twenty poles to a Black Gum thence north seventy degrees east at seventy poles fifteen poles at one hundred & twenty one and one hundred & sixty six poles to a Dogwood hickory and red oak on the side of a hill thence south seventy one degrees east at ninety six the aforesaid River all one hundred and ninety six poles to two hickory and white oak saplins thence south fifty one degrees east one hundred and eighty poles to several marked trees thence north fifty seven degrees west three hundred and twenty four poles to the satisfaction with all houses barns and buildings gardens orchards pastures meadows fields ways waters water courses easements emoluments and all yearly rents issues and profits from henceforth due or arriving and all other advantages & commodities to the same and all and every or any part or parcell thereof in any wise belonging or appertaining and the reversion and reversions and remainder and remainders of the land and of every part and

p. <u>Louisa County Deed Book A 11h July 1743</u>

89 thereof To Have and To Hold the said above granted and sold land and premises with their and every of their appurtenances unto the said ANDREW ROE his heirs and assigns to his only proper use and behoof of the said ANDREW ROE and of his heirs and assigns forever and the said JOHN THOMPSON for himself his heirs Executors and Administrators and every of them doth covenant and agree to and with the said ROE his heirs and assigns in manner and form following that is to say that the said THOMPSON now is and rightfully and lawfully possessed of the said above granted and sold Land and premises with the appurtenances of his own just and proper right in fee simple and that he hath good & lawful power and absolute authority to sell and convey the land to the said ANDREW ROE his heirs and assigns and that it shall and may be lawfull to and for the said ROE his heirs and assigns and that it shall and may be lawful to and for the said ROE his heirs and assigns and every of them from time to time and at all times forever hereafter peaceably to have hold use occupy possess and enjoy all and singular the said above

granted and sold Land and premises with their & every of their appurtenances and thereof all other and former of other sales or deeds of sale bargains conveyances mortgages rights of Dower intails suits evictions or hinderances or molestations whatsoever and that he the said THOMPSON his Executors and Administrators and every of them the above granted and sold Land and premises with the appurtenances unto the said ROE his heirs and assigns against all other persons whatsoever will forever warrant defend and the said THOMPSON by these presents for himself his heirs Exors. and Admors. and every of them doth further covenant and promise grant and agree to and with the said ROE his heirs and assigns that ANNE his wife of the said THOMPSON is not able to travel to the Court of the said County of Louisa by means of the great distance she lives therefrom that she might relinquish her right of Dower of in and to the promises and every part thereof with the appurtenances shall remain free clear from her the said ANNE's right of Dower or thereto which she shall or by any means or ways whatsoever she shall or may have and that the said ANDREW ROE his heirs and assigns shall and may forever hereafter and peaceably enjoy the said premises above granted with the appurtenances and from her the said ANNE's right and title of Dower above mentioned shall or any hereditaments or imcumbrances any ways happening or arising about the same. In Witness whereof the said parties to those presents their hands and seals have fixed this day and year first above written.

Sealed and delivered (the words containing by JOHN THOMPSON [seal]
affirmation five hundred & twenty four acres
to the same more or less first interlined in presence of
R. FORD, JOHN JOYCE, THOMAS WILLIAMSON, ABRAHM. VENABLE, JO. BICKLEY, THOMAS PAULETT, BENJA. HOUSTON

p. <u>Louisa County Deed Book A 11th July 1743</u>

90 Memo. of Mr. ANDREW ROE the ninth day of March 174 2/3 the sum of thirty five pounds current money of Virginia being the consideration money for the within granted and sold Land and premises according to the true intent and meaning of the within deed I say received of me. JOHN THOMPSON

Test R. FORD, JOHN JOYCE, THOMAS WILLIAMSON, ABRAHM. VENABLE, JO. BICKLEY, THOMAS PAULETT, BENJA. HOUSTON

Memorandum that on the day and year within mentioned peaceable and quietly seisin and possession of the within mentioned Land and premises with the appurtenances was had and taken by the within named JOHN THOMPSON and by him delivered to the within named ROE for the use of the said ROE and of his heirs and assigns according to the Tenor purport and true meaning of the within deed. JOHN THOMPSON

In presence of R. FORD, JOHN JOYCE, THOMAS WILLIAMSON, ABRAHM. VENABLE, JO. BICKLEY, THOMAS PAULETT, BENJA. HOUSTON

At a Court held for Louisa County on Monday the XIth day of July 1743.
This Indenture receipt and Memorandum of livery of seisen were this day in open Court acknowledged by JOHN THOMPSON to be his Act and Deeds & by the Court admitted to record and is ordered. Test JAS. LITTLEPAGE, Clk Truly recorded

-This Indenture made the eleventh day of July in the year of our Lord God one thousand seven hundred and forty three and in the seventeenth year of the Reign of our Sovereign Lord George the second by the grace of God of Great Britain, France and Ireland King Defender of the Faith. Between WILLIAM BURRUS of the parish of St. Margret in the County of Caroline of the one part and JOHN STARKE of the parish of Fredricksville and County of Louisa of the other part. Witnesseth that the said WILLIAM BURRUS for and in consideration of the sum of twenty six pounds current money of Virginia to him in hand already paid by the said JOHN STARKE the receipt whereof he the said WILLIAM BURRUS doth hereby acknowledge himself to be fully satisfied contented thereof and every part and parcel thereof doth for himself his heirs Exrs. and Admrs. acquit and discharge the said JOHN STARKE his heirs Exrs. and Admrs. by these presents Hath granted bargained sold transferred and confirmed and by these presents doth grant bargain sell transfer and confirm unto the said JOHN

p. <u>Louisa County Deed Book A 11th July 1743</u>

91 STARKE his heirs Exrs. Admrs. and assigns forever and certain tenement tract or parcel of land containing four hundred acres situate and being in Fredericksville parish and in the County of Louisa on both sides of the north fork of MOREMAN's River and bounded as followeth [to wit] beginning at Major HENRY's corner white oak and chestnut tree running thence north six degrees west fifty six a branch in all one hundred and sixty two poles to a chestnut tree thence north twenty degrees east at fifty three a branch in all one hundred and fourty poles to a hickory saplin and sassafras tree thence south fifty eight degrees east one hundred and fifty nine to the north fork of MOREMAN's River at two hundred and six the same at four hundred and ten a branch in all four hundred and thirty eight poles to a red oak saplin thence south thirty five degrees rejoining MOREMAN's River to Major HENRY's corner two white oak saplins and thence along his line north fifty five degrees west two hundred and six poles to the beginning To Have and To Hold the said four hundred acres of Land and premises to there more or less within the aforesaid bounds with the appurtenances together with all houses, buildings edifices orchards gardens fences woods waters watercourses profits commodities emoluments and advantages whatsoever to the same belonging or in any wise appertaining to the said JOHN STARKE his heirs and assigns forever and to no other use intent or purpose whatsoever and the said WILLIAM BURRUS now is and standeth lawfully seised of and in the said tenement tract or parcel of land and premises with the appurtenances of a good sure perfect and indefeasable estate in fee simple and now hath good right full power and lawful authority to grant convey the said tenement tract or parcel of land and premises with their appurtenances and meaning of those presents and that it shall and may be lawfull for the said JOHN STARKE his heirs Exors. Admrs. and assigns from time to time and at all times forever hereafter peaceably and quietly to have hold use occupy and enjoy the said tenement tract or parcel of land and premises with the appurtenances without the Lot suit Trouble or interruption of him the said WILLIAM BURRUS his heirs Exros. Admrs. of assigns or any other person or persons

whatsoever claiming or to claim any right title interest or demand of in or unto the said tenement tract or parcel of land and all singular other the premises with these appurtenances by from or under him his heirs Exrs. and Admrs. or any or either of them discharged from all manner of incumbrances whatsoever the Quitrents henceforth growing due and payable to our Sovereign the King his heirs and successors only excepted and foreprized and the said WILLIAM BURRUS his heirs Exors. and Admrs. by these presents doth covenant and grant for with the said JOHN STARKE and his heirs and assigns that he the said WILLIAM BURRUS shall and will from time to time and at all times forever hereafter upon reasonable request and at the charges in the Law of the said JOHN

p. <u>Louisa County Deed Book A 11th July 1743</u>

92 STARKE his heirs Exrs. Admrs. and assigns to make and execute or raise or promise to made done and execute all and every such act and acts thing and things conveyances and assurances in the Law whatsoever for the further and more better and perfect conveying and sure making the said tenement tract or parcel of land as shall be reasonably devised advised or required by him them or any or either of them or any of their council learned in the law and the said WILLIAM BURRUS for himself his heirs Exors. Admrs. and assigns the said tenement tract or parcel of land unto the said JOHN STARKE his heirs Exrs. Admrs. and assigns and will forever warrant and defend by these presents from the claim challenge or demand of any person or persons whatsoever and the said WILLIAM BURRUS for himself his heirs Exrs. and Admrs. doth covenant and grant to and with the said JOHN STARKE his heirs Exrs. Admrs. and assigns that the said tenement tract or parcel of land as free and clear from all manner of Sailes deeds Leases Joyntors mortgages extents judgments exenitions and incumbrances whatsoever and that the said WILLIAM BURRUS his heirs Exrs. and Admrs. shall and will acknowledge this his deed in Louisa County Court unto the said JOHN STARKE his heirs Exrs. Admrs. or assigns when the cause required. In Witness whereof I have hereunto set my hand and seal the day and year first above written.

Signed sealed and delivered
in the presence of W. BURRUS [seal]

JOHN FORD, WM. THOMPSON, JAMES X [his mark] ROACH

Memorandum that on the eleventh day of July in the year of our Lord God one thousand seven hundred and fourty three full and reasonable possession and seisen of all and singular the Lands and tenements and hereditaments within granted or mentioned to be granted was delivered by the said WILLIAM BURRUS unto the said JOHN STARKE to hold to the said JOHN STARKE his heirs Exrs. Admors and assigns forever according to the force form and effort of this deed in the presence of

JOHN FORD, WM. THOMPSON, JAMES X [his mark] ROACH WILLIAM BURRUS

At a Court held for Louisa County on Monday the XIth day of July 1743.
This Indenture and Memorandum of livery of seisin were this day in open Court acknowledged by WILLIAM BURRUS to be his act & deed by the Court admitted to record and is recorded. Test JAS. LITTLEPAGE, Clk.

-This Indenture made the fifth day of August in the Seventeenth year of the reign of our Sovereign Lord George the second by the Grace of God of Great Britain France and Ireland King Defender of the faith &c. Anno Domo. one thousand seven hundred and fourty three. Between JOHN MacGEHEE's of Saint Martin's parish in the County of Louisa of the one part and THOMAS POINDEXTER of the said parish and county of the other part. Witnesseth that the said JOHN MacGEHEE for and

p. <u>Louisa County Deed Book A 8th August 1743</u>

93 in consideration of the sum of five shillings of lawful money of England to him in hand paid by the said THOMAS POINDEXTER the receipt whereof he doth hereby acknowledge hath bargained and by these presents doth bargain and sell unto the said THOMAS POINDEXTER all that plantation that the said THOMAS POINDEXTER now lives together with one hundred acres of land adjoining the said plantation lying and being in the parish and County aforesaid with all houses edifices buildings and tenements & all gardens woods ways and water courses whatsoever therein or thereunto belonging or in any wise appertaining and bounded as followeth beginning at a corner Red Oak of WILLIAM WILLONS in THOMAS GRAVES line runing along the land north thirty five degrees east eighty seven poles to a corner red oak on the south side of great Rocky Creek then down the same making in a strait line thirty two poles to a corner maple on the north side the said Creek thence north three and a half degrees east twenty five poles to a great white oak thence north fifteen degrees west fifty eight poles to white oak thence north eighty degrees west one hundred and seven poles to two white oaks by the side of a glade thence south eighty eight degrees west one hundred and ten poles to a hickory and white oak saplin in JOHN MacGEHEE and WILLIAM WILLONS line on the south side of a hill then along the said line south fourty five degrees east one hundred and eighty eight poles to the beginning place and the Reversion and reversions remainder and remainders of the said Land as before described To Have and To Hold the said one hundred acres of Land as before related & all and singular other the premises herein mentioned intended to be hereby bargained & sold with their every of their appurtenances unto the said THOMAS POINDEXTER his Exrs. and assigns from the day before the date hereof for and during the form of one whole year from thence next ensuing and fully to be ended yielding and paying therefore the yearly rent of one pepper corn at the season of St. Michael the Arch Angel only if the same be demanded to the intent that by virtue of these presents and of the statues for transferring uses into possession the said THOMAS POINDEXTER may by in the actual possession of the premises and do enable to grant of the Reversions and inheritances thereof to him and his heirs forever. In Witness whereof the said JOHN MacGEHEE hath hereunto set his hand and seal the day and year first above written.

Signed sealed and delivered
in the presence of JOHN MacGEHEE [seal]
DAN BURFORD, JN. PRYOR, JO. BICKLEY

At a Court held for Louisa County on Monday the 8th day of August 1743.
This Indenture was this day in open Court acknowledged by JOHN MacGEHEE as his act &

deed by the Court admitted to record and is recorded. Test JAM. LITTLEPAGE
This day also at ANNE the wife of the said JOHN MacGEHEE being first privily examined as the law directs & delivering her consent thereto, did in open Court relinquish unto THOMAS

p. Louisa County Deed Book A 8th August 1743
94 POINDEXTER the right of Dower which she hath in the Land the Indenture and the same by the Court was admitted to record & is recorded. Test JAS. LITTLEPAGE, Clk.

-This Indenture made the fifth day of August in the Seventeenth year of the reign of our Sovereign Lord George the second by the Grace of God of Great Britain France and Ireland King Defender of the faith &c. Anno Domo. one thousand seven hundred and fourty three. Between JOHN MacGEHEE's of Saint Martin's parish in the County of Louisa of the one part and THOMAS POINDEXTER of the said parish and county of the other part. Witnesseth that for and in consideration of the sum of twenty five pounds current money of Virginia to the said JOHN MacGEHEE in hand paid by the said THOMAS POINDEXTER at or before the ensealing and delivery of these presents the receipt whereof he doth hereby acknowledge and thereof and of every part and parcell thereof doth clearly acquit and discharge the said THOMAS POINDEXTER his heirs Exrs. and Admrs. and every of them by these presents the said JOHN MacGEHEE hath granted aliened released and confirmed and by these presents doth grant alien release and confirm unto the said THOMAS POINDEXTER in his actual possession more being by virtue of a bargain and sale to him thereof made for one whole year by Indenture bearing date the day before the date hereof and by the force of the Statute for transferring uses into possession all that plantation whereon the said THOMAS POINDEXTER now lives together with one hundred acres of Land adjoining to the said plantation lying and being in the parish and County aforesaid with all houses edifices buildings and tenements and all gardens woods ways and water courses whatsoever therein or thereunto belonging or in any wise appertaining and bounded as followeth beginning at a corner Red Oak of WILLIAM WILLONS in THOMAS GRAVES line runing along the land north thirty five degrees east eighty seven poles to a corner red oak on the south side of great Rocky Creek then down the same making in a strait line thirty two poles to a corner maple on the north side the said Creek thence north three and a half degrees east twenty five poles to a great white oak thence north fifteen degrees west fifty eight poles to white oak thence north eighty degrees west one hundred and seven poles to two white oaks by the side of a glade thence south eighty eight degrees west one hundred and ten poles to a hickory and white oak saplin in JOHN MacGEHEE and WILLIAM WILLONS line on the south side of a hill then along the said line south fourty five degrees east one hundred and eighty eight poles to the beginning place and the Reversion and reversions remainder and remainders of the said Land as before described To Have and To Hold the said one hundred acres of Land as before set forth & all and singular other the premises herein before mentioned and intended to be hereby granted with the appurtenances unto the said THOMAS POINDEXTER his heirs to the side of the said THOMAS POINDEXTER and of his heirs and assigns forever and the said JOHN MacGEHEE for himself his heirs Exrs. and Admrs.

doth covenant and grant to and with the said THOMAS POINDEXTER his heirs and assigns by

p. Louisa County Deed Book A 8th August 1743

95 these presents that the said JOHN MacGEHEE now is and standeth lawfully and rightly seisen of the said one hundred acres of Land as before aforesaid with all the appurtenances of a good sure and perfect absolute and indefeasible estate in fee simple and now hath good and full power and lawfull and absolute authority to grant and convey the said one hundred acres of land and premises unto the said THOMAS POINDEXTER and his heirs according to the purport true intent meaning of these presents and that it shall and may be lawfull to and for the said THOMAS POINDEXTER his heirs and assigns from time to time and at all times forever hereafter peaceably and quietly to have and to hold occupy possess and enjoy the said one hundred acres of land as before set forth and all and singular other the premises herein before mentioned and intended to be hereby granted with the appurtenances without any Lawfully Lot suit Trouble or interruption of him the said JOHN MacGEHEE his heirs or assigns or any other person or persons whatsoever of or from any other person or persons lawfully claiming or to claim in by from or under him them or and of them discharged of and from all incumbrances whatsoever rents from henceforth to grow due and payable to the Lord or Lords of the fee or fees of the premises for and in respect of his or their excepted and foreprized and the said JOHN MacGEHEE for him and his heirs the said one hundred acres of land as before specified and other the premises with the appurtenances unto the said THOMAS POINDEXTER and his heirs against him the said JOHN MacGEHEE and his heirs all claiming or to claim in by from or under him them or any of them or in by from or under any other person or persons whatsoever shall and will warrant and forever by these presents. In Witness whereof the said JOHN MacGEHEE hath hereunto set his hand seal the day and year first above written.

Signed sealed and delivered
in presence of JOHN MACKGEHEE [seal]
DANL. BURFORD, JN. PRYOR, JO. BICKLEY

At a Court held for Louisa County on Monday the VIIIth day of August 1743.
This Indenture was this day in open Court acknowledged by JOHN MACKGEHEE to be his Act and Deed and by the Court admitted to record and is recorded.
This day also ANNE the wife of the said JOHN MACKGEHEE being first privily examined as the Law directs & delivering her consent thereto, did in open Court relinquish unto THOMAS POINDEXTER the right of Dower which she hath in the Land the Indenture and the same by the Court was admitted to record & is recorded. Test JAS. LITTLEPAGE, Clk.

-This Indenture made this VIIIth day of June in the year of our Lord MDCCXLIII and Between JOHN SMITHSON of the one part and ELIZABETH SMITHSON his wife of the other part. Witnesseth that for and in consideration of the above ELIZABETH being his well beloved wife the said SMITHSON hath thought still to lend unto the said ELIZABETH SMITHSON divining the form of her natural life, a dividend of his estate as followeth, to wit, one negroe man named PETER and one feather bed and furniture and do by the above mentioned premises warrant and defend the said negro and bed and furniture to be good and valliable unto the said ELIZABETH SMITHSON during the above mentioned form from all demands claims wrights or titles whatsoever by any person or persons whatsoever. In Witness whereof I have hereunto set my hand and seal the day and year above written.

Signed sealed and delivered in presence of us

WILLIAM OGILVIE, A. J. SMITH JN. SMITHSON

p. Louisa County Deed Book A 8th August 1743

96 At a Court held for Louisa County on Monday the VIIIth day of August 1743.

This Indenture was this day in open Court acknowledged by JOHN SMITHSON to be his Act & Deed by the Court admitted to record and is recorded.

Test JAS. LITTLEPAGE, Clk. Truly recorded.

-This Indenture made the eighth day of August in the seventeenth year of the reign of our Sovereign Lord George the second by the Grace of God of Great Britain France and Ireland King Defender of the faith &c. and in the year of our Lord 1743. Between BENJAMIN BROWN of the County of Hanover of the one part and JAMES YANCEY of the County of Louisa of the other part. Witnesseth that the said BENJAMIN BROWN for and in consideration of the sum of six pounds current money to him in hand already paid satisfied hath given granted and by these presents doth absolutely alien enfeoff and grant unto the said JAMES YANCEY his heirs and assigns forever one certain tract or parcell of land lying and being in Louisa County on the north side of a north branch of the Little River called by the name of Elk Branch in the parish of St. Martin's containing fifty acres and bounded as followeth Vizt. Beginning at a corner poplar runing thence north forty two west thirty four poles thence north fifty five west seventy poles to a corner pine thence north fifty east ninety four poles to a corner pine thence forty two & a half east eighty eight poles to a corner of three small maples standing on the north side of the said Elk branch thence down the said branch south forty two west eighty poles to the beginning with all appurtenances whatsoever in any wise thereunto appertaining To Have and To Hold the said Land and all and singular other the premises unto the said JAMES YANCEY his heirs and assigns forever and that in as firm and ample manner to all intents and purposes as an estate in fee simple absolute and to hold or enjoy and such an estate in to the premises the said BENJAMIN BROWN by this deed binds and obliges himself his heirs Exors. Admrs. to warrant and forever defend to be good and valid to the said JAMES YANCEY his heirs or assigns forever against all manner of persons claiming under or any pretense right or title whatsoever and also that the said BENJAMIN BROWN his heirs &c. shall and will make and defend such other goods for the better conveying the premises by the true meaning of this deed unto the said JAMES YANCEY his heirs and assigns forever as by him them or their council shall be required and to the true keeping and fullfilling of all and singular the premises or titles and conditions of this deed the said BENJAMIN BROWN binds and obliges himself his heirs or assigns in the penal sum of fifty pounds current money. In Witness whereof the said BENJAMIN BROWN hath hereunto set his hand and seal the day and year first above written signed sealed and

delivered in the presence of us [blank] BENJAMIN BROWN [seal]
Memorandum that upon the 8th day of August full and peaceable possession and seisin was given and delivered by the within named BENJAMIN BROWN of the within mentioned dividend of land with the appurtenances unto the within named JAMES YANCEY for and unto his use his heirs and assigns forever according to the true purport of this Indenture in presence of us Witnesses [blank] BENJAMIN BROWN

p. <u>Louisa County Deed Book A 8th August 1743</u>
97 At a Court held for Louisa County on Monday the 8th day of August 1743.

This Indenture and Memorandum of livery of seisin were this day in open Court acknowledged by BENJAMIN BROWN to be his Act & Deed & by the Court admitted to record and is recorded. Test JAS. LITTLEPAGE, Clk.

-This Indenture made this Eighth day of August in the year of our Lord Christ One thousand seven hundred and forty three. Between JOHN RED of Louisa County of the one part and WILLIAM BALLARD of Caroline County of the other part. Witnesseth that the said JOHN RED for and in consideration of the sum of Twenty five pounds current money of Virginia to him in hand paid by the said WILLIAM BALLARD at and before the ensealing and delivery of these presents the receipt whereof he doth hereby acknowledge and thereof and of every part and parcel thereof the same doth clearly acquit and discharge the said WILLIAM BALLARD his Executors & Administrators and Every of them by these presents hath granted aliened released enfeoffed and confirmed and by these presents for the consideration above set down doth grant alien release enfeoff and perpetually confirm unto the said WILLIAM BALLARD and to his heirs and assigns forever all that the JOHN RED his Parcel or Tract of Land containing four hundred acres lying and being on both sides Naked Creek in the said County of Louisa and Bounded as followeth [to wit] Beginning at JOHN ROGERS corner Pointer's in Major HENRY's line runing thence along the same North one hundred & forty four poles to Pointers in HENRY's line, thence on a New line north fifty one degrees east at twenty a branch in all two hundred and sixty three poles to a pine in Major HENRY's line thence on the same south twenty seven degrees east three hundred and eight poles to JOHN ROGER's Corner Pointers and thereon his line south eighty four degrees west three hundred and forty seven poles to the beginning and all the estate right title interest use property and claim of him the said JOHN RED his heirs or assigns of in or unto the premises and the Reversion and reversions Remainder and Remainders Yearly and other Rents and profits of the premises and of every part and parcel thereof To Have and To Hold the said four hundred acres of Land above bounded and all and singular other the premises herein before mentioned and intended to be hereby granted with their and every of their appurtenances unto the said WILLIAM BALLARD and his heirs to the only use and behoof of him the said WILLIAM BALLARD and to his heirs and assigns forever and the said JOHN RED for himself his heirs Executors and Administrators doth covenant and grant to and with the said WILLIAM BALLARD his heirs and assigns by the said presents that he the said JOHN RED now is and standeth lawfully and Rightfully Seised of and in the said four hundred acres of Land above Bounded of a good true profit absolute and indefeasable estate in fee simple and Now hath good right full Power and Lawfull and Absolute Authority to grant and convey the Land according to the Purport True Intent and Meaning of these presents and it shall and that it shall and May be Lawfull to and for the said WILLIAM BALLARD his heirs and assigns from time to time and at all times forever hereafter peaceably and quietly to have & hold occupy possess and enjoy the said four hundred acres of land and all and singular other the premises herein before mentioned and intended to be hereby granted with their and every of their appurtenances without

p. Louisa County Deed Book A 8th August 1743
98 the Lawfull Lot Suit Trouble or Molestation of him the said JOHN RED his heirs or assigns or any other person or persons Whatsoever Discharged and from all Incumbrances or Evictions Whatsoever the Quitrents from henceforth to grow due to our Sovereign Lord the King his heirs and Successors, only Excepted and foreprized, and the said JOHN RED for himself his heirs Executors and Administrators the aforesaid granted premises with their appurtenances unto the said WILLIAM BALLARD and his heirs and all claiming or to claim Right, in by from or under him them or any of them or any other person or persons whatsoever, Have and will warrant and forever Defend by these presents. In Witness whereof the said JOHN RED to these presents hath Interchangeably set his hand and affixed his seal the day and year first above written.

Signed sealed and Delivered in presence of [blank] JOHN RED [seal]

Memorandum that Peaceable and quiet possession of the within mentioned premises was first had and taken by the within named JOHN RED and by him given to the within named WILLIAM BALLARD by the Delivery of Turf and Twigg of the Ground of the said Land as the usual Symbolls of Livery and Seisin to be by him hath according to the within written Indentures. In Witness whereof the said JOHN RED hath hereunto set his hand and seal this eighth day of August 1743. JOHN RED [seal]

At a Court held for Louisa County on Monday the 8th day of August 1743.

This Indenture and Memorandum of Livery of Seisin was this day in open court acknowledged by JOHN RED to be his Act and Deed and by the Court admitted to record and is recorded. Test JAS. LITTLEPAGE, Clk.

This day also MARY the wife of the said JOHN RED being first privily examined as the Law Directs and declaring her consent thereto did in open Court relinquish unto WILLIAM BALLARD the Right of Dower Which she hath in the Land conveyed by this Indenture the Court was admitted to Record and is Recorded. Test JAS. LITTLEPAGE, Clk.

-This Indenture made this eighth day of August in the year of our Lord 1743 By and Between HENRY BAILEY of the one part and JOHN RAGLAND of the other part XXXXXXX. Witness that the said BAILEY hath for and in the consideration of the sum of twenty pounds of Virginia currency to him in hand allread paide and satisfied hath given granted and by these presents doth absolutely aleind the

p. Louisa County Deed Book A 8th August 1743

99 use of and grant unto the said RAGLAND his heirs and assigns forever 400 acres of land lying and being as is Described in a paten Bareing date February the Ninth one thousand seven hundred and thirty seven with all Maner, and all Singular the Members Wrights and Hereditaments and appurtenances Whatsoever Together with all and every Deeds Wrighting and Evidence to the said 400 acres of Land be the same more or less according to the Bounds thereof or to any part or parcel their of in any wise appertaining To Have and To Hold the said 400 acres of Land and all and Singular other the premises unto the said RAGLAND his heirs and assigns forever and that in as firm ample maner to all Intents and porposis as an Estate in fee simple absolutely ran be held or Injoyed and such an estate in and for the premises the said BAILEY binds & obliges himself his heirs and assigns by this Deeds to Warrant and forever defend to be good and Vallied unto the said RAGLAND his heirs and assigns forever against all Maner of persons claiming under any Progems Wright or title Whatsoever and also that the said BAILEY his heirs and assigns shall execute shuch other deeds and assurances for the better conveying the premises by the True Meaning of this Deeds unto the said RAGLAND and to the punktiall performance true keeping and fulfiling and Singular the premises artickols claims and conditions of this Deeds the said BAILEY binds and oblidges himself his heirs Executors Administrators and assigns in the penal sum of five hundred pounds curant money of Virginia. In Witness the said BAILEY hath hereunto set his hand and seale the day and year above written.

Signed Sealed and Delivered
In the presence of HENRY BAYLY [seal]
JR. SMITHSON, JAMES LASSLY

Memorandum that upon the [blank] full and peaceable possession and seisure was given and Delivered by the within named BAILEY of the within mentioned 400 acres of Land and of the appurtenances thereunto belonging unto the within named RAGLAND for and unto the use of him his heirs and assigns forever, according to the true purport of this Indenture.

In presence of us JR. SMITHSON, JAMES LASLEY HENRY BAYLEY

p. Louisa County Deed Book A 8th August 1743

100 At a Court held for Louisa County on Monday the Eighth day of August 1743.

This Indenture and Memorandum of Livery of Seisin was this day in open Court acknowledged by HENRY BAILEY to be his Act and Deed and by the court admitted to record and is Recorded. Test JAS. LITTLEPAGE, Clk.

-This Indenture made the third day of May in the year of our Lord Christ one thousand seven hundred and forty three Between DAVID MILLS in the County of Louisa of the one part and BENJAMIN BROWN of the County of Hanover of the other part. Witnesseth that the said DAVID MILLS for and in consideration of one hundred and forty pounds current money of Virginia to him in hand paid before the signing and sealing of these presents the receipt whereof he doth hereby confess and acknowledge and himself therewith fully satisfied contented and paid and of every part and parcell Thereof hath bargained and sold and doth by these presents Bargain and Sell make over and Confirm unto him the said BENJAMIN BROWN his heirs or assigns one certain tract or parcel of Land containing by estimation two thousand eight hundred and fifty acres be the same more or less situate lying and being in the County of Louisa on the North fork of MORMANS River and bounded as followeth to wit Beginning at a White oak saplin near the River of the Lower side the River runing thence North one thousand and twenty poles to a former white oak saplin near the River on the upper side of the said River 6 hours North sixty degrees west two hundred and six poles to a white oak and chestnut tree on a Ridge 8 hours south forty Degrees West five hundred and eight poles to two white oaks thence south fifteen Degrees West four hundred and thirty seven poles to a Chestnut saplin in the County line 6 hours along the same south sixty five Degrees east six hundred and ninety poles to the Beginning To Have and To Hold and peaceably to enjoy the aforesaid two thousand eight hundred and fifty acres of Land with all the premises and appurtenances thereto belonging from the claims Right or Title of him the said DAVID MILLS his heirs or assigns or any person or person Whatsoever to the only proper use and behoof of him the said BENJAMIN BROWN his heirs or assigns forever and the said DAVID

p. <u>Louisa County Deed Book A 8th August 1743</u>

101 MILLS for himself his heirs and Administrators doth covenant promise and agree that he will from time to time and at all times forever hereafter against all person Whatsoever the Right of the above said Land and premises warrant and defend to the said BENJAMIN BROWN his heirs and assigns and that he shall and will be Ready at any time Hereafter to make any further Right or Title or Conveyance that he the said BENJAMIN BROWN or his Council in the Law shall Require in Witness whereof I have hereunto set my hand and seal the day and year above written.

Signed Sealed and Delivered In presence of [blank] DAVID MILLS [seal]

Memorandum that full and peaceable possession and Seizen was this day given and Delivered by the within mentioned DAVID MILLS to BENJAMIN BROWN of the Land and premises within mentioned in presence of us whose Hands are Subscribed. In Witness whereof the said DAVID MILLS hath of his Hand and Seal the day and year within mentioned.

Test DAVID MILLS [seal]

At a Court held for Louisa County on Monday the 8th day of August 1743.
This Indenture and Memorandum of Livery of Seisin was this day in open Court acknowledged by DAVID MILLS to be his Act and Deed and by the Court admitted to Record and is Recorded. Test JAS. LITTLEPAGE, Clk.

-This Indenture made this twelfth of September in the year of our Lord Christ 1743. Between WILLIAM CRADOCK of the parish of Fredicks in the county of Louisa of the one part and MICHAEL HOLLAND of the parish of Saint Paul in the County of Hanover of the other part. Witnesseth that the said WILLIAM CRADOCK for and in consideration of the sum of forty two pounds current money to him in hand paid by the said MICHAEL HOLLAND at and before the Inseasing and Delivery of these presents the Receipt Whereof he doth hereby acknowledge and therefore and every parcell of the same doth hereby acquit and Discharge the said MICHAEL HOLLAND his heirs Executors and Administrators and Every of them by these presents for the consideration above set down doth grant alien Release Enfeoffe and Perpetually Confirm unto the said MICHAEL BALLARD and to his heirs and assigns forever all that the said WILLIAM CRADOCK his parcell or Tract of Land containing four hundred acres Lying and being in

p. Louisa County Deed Book A 12th September 1743

102 the parish in the aforesaid County of Louisa and on the west side of the first Mountain and is Bonded as follows [to wit] Beginning at a small pine of the side of a Hill and runing thence south forty six Degrees east at one hundred and twenty two, a Branch at two hundred; and two hundred and seven poles two more Branches in all three hundred and twenty poles to three white oak saplins thence North forty four Degrees east at Sixty four a Branch in all two hundred poles to several pines; thence forty six Degrees west at one hundred and twenty eight Branch in all three hundred and twenty poles to a pine thence South forty four Degrees west two hundred poles to the Beginning and Estate Right Title Interest use property and claims of him the said MICHAEL HOLLAND of in or unto the premises and the Reversion and Reversions Remainder and Remainders yearly and other rents and profits of the premises and of every part and parcell thereof To Have and To Hold the said four hundred acres of Land above bounded and all and singular other premises herein before Mentioned & Intended to be hereby granted unto the said MICHAEL HOLLAND and his heirs for the only use and Behoof of him the said MICHAEL HOLLAND his heirs and assigns forever, and the said WILLIAM CRADOCK and for himself his Executors Administrators doth covenant and grant to which the said MICHAEL HOLLAND his heirs and assigns by these presents that he the said WILLIAM CRADOCK now is and Standeth Lawfull and Rightfully Seized of and in the said four hundred acres of Land above bounded and premises with their appurtenances of a good True perfect absolute and Indefeasible Estate in fee simple and now hath good Right full and absolute authority to grant and convey the Land according to the purported Intent and Meaning of these presents and that is shall and May be Lawfull to and for the said MICHAEL HOLLAND his heirs and assigns from time to time and at all times for ever hereafter peaceable and Quietly to have hold occupy possess use and Enjoy the said four hundred acres of Land above bounded and all and Singular other premises herein before mentioned and

p. Louisa County Deed Book A 12th September 1743

103 Intended to be hereby granted with their appurtenances without any Lawfull lot suit Trouble or Interruption of him the said WILLIAM CRADOCK his heirs or assigns or any other person or persons Whatsoever Discharged of and from all Incumbrances or Evictions Whatsoever the Quitrents from hence forth to grow due to our Sovereign Lord the King his heirs Successors only Excepted and foreprized and the said WILLIAM CRADOCK for himself his heirs Executors & Administrators the above bounded four hundred acres of Land and premises with these appurtenances unto the said MICHAEL HOLLAND his heirs against the

said WILLIAM CRADOCK and his heirs & all claiming or to claim Right in by from or under them or any of them or any other person or persons whatsoever shall and will warrant forever Defend by these presents In Witness whereof

Signed Sealed and Delivered In the presence of

A.J. SMITH, ROBERT WATSON WILLIAM X [his mark] CRADOCK [seal]

Memorandum that peaceable and Quiet possession of the within mentioned premises was first had and taken by the within named WILLIAM CRADDOCK and by him Delivered to the within named MICHAEL HOLLAND by the Delivery of Turf and Twigg of the Ground of the said Land as the usual Symbolls of Livery of Seisin to be by him held according to the within Indenture. In Presence of

A.J. SMITH, ROBERT WATSON WILLIAM X [his mark] CRADOCK

Twelfth day of September 1743. Received of the within named MICHAEL HOLLAND the sum of forty five pounds Current money being the consideration within mentioned Witness my hand the day and year above written.

A.J. SMITH, ROBERT WATSON WILLIAM X [his mark] CRADOCK

At a Court held for Louisa County on Monday the 12th day of September 1743.
This Indenture Receipt and Memorandum of Livery of Seisin was this day in open Court acknowledged by WILLIAM CRADOCK to be his Act and Deed and by the Court admitted to Record and is Recorded. Test JAS. LITTLEPAGE, Clk.

This day also MARY the wife of the said WILLIAM being first privily examined as the Law directs & declaring her consent thereto did in open Court Relinquish unto MICHAEL HOLLAND the Right of Dower which she hath in the Land conveyed by this indenture and the Land by the Court was admitted to Record and is Recorded. Test JAS. LITTLEPAGE, Clk.

p. <u>Louisa County Deed Book A 12th September 1743</u>

104 -This Indenture made the fifth day of August in the year of our Lord Christ one thousand seven hundred and forty three Between JOHN WATSON of the parish of Fredricksville in the County of Louisa of the one part and JOHN RICHARDSON of the parish and County aforesaid of the other part. Witness that the said JOHN WATSON for and in consideration of the sum of ten pounds current money of Virginia to him in hand paid by the said JOHN RICHARDSON the Receipt Whereof he the said JOHN WATSON do hereby acknowledge he the said JOHN WATSON have granted bargained and sold aliened and confirmed and by these presents do grant bargain and sell alien and confirm unto the said JOHN RICHARDSON his heirs and assigns for ever all that Tract or parcel of Land and plantation thereon situate lying being in the said parish of Fredricksvile in the County aforesaid containing sixty acres be the same more or less it being part of the Land whereon the said JOHN WATSON now lives and Bounded as followeth to wit Beginning at a Spanish oak saplin on a small branch runing thence south fourty one degrees east fifty poles thence south four degrees east one hundred poles thence south fifty five west six poles thence north seventy six west one hundred and two poles thence North forty three east to the beginning and also all Trees woods underwoods Tiths Commons and commons of pastures profits commodities advantages hereditaments waies watercourses appurtenances

whatsoever to the said sixty acres of Land and Plantation above mentioned belonging or any wise appertaining and also the Reversion reversions Remainder and Remainders Rents of these and every part thereof and all the Estate Right Title Interest claiming and Demand Whatsoever of him the said JOHN WATSON of in and to the said Tract or parcel of sixty acres of Land with the said plantation thereon and premises and every part with the appurtenances unto the said JOHN RICHARDSON his heirs and assigns to the only proper use and behoof of the said JOHN RICHARDSON his heirs and assigns for ever and the said JOHN WATSON for himself and his heirs the said Tract or parcel of Land sixty acres of Land and premises and every part thereof against him and his heirs and against all and every other person or persons Whatsoever to the said JOHN RICHARDSON for his heirs and assigns shall and will warrant and forever Defend by these presents In Witness whereof I the said JOHN WATSON have hereunto set my Hand and Seal the day and year first above written. Signed Sealed and Delivered
In the presence of us JOHN WATSON [seal]

p. Louisa County Deed Book A 12th September 1743
105 Memorandum that on the 5th day of August 1743 peaceable and quiet possession was had and taken by the within named JOHN WATSON of the within granted Land and premises and the Land was by him delivered unto the within named JOHN RICHARDSON as the usual symbols of Livery and Seizen according to the foresaid form & effort of the within Deed. In presence of [blank] JOHN WATSON [seal]
5th August 1743 Then Recording the sums of ten pounds current money of Virginia it being the consideration money for the Lands and premises within granted received the Land of the within named JOHN RICHARDSON pd. me.
At a Court held for Louisa County on Monday the 12th day of September.
This Indenture Receipt and Memorandum of Livery of seisen was this day in open Court acknowledged by JOHN WATSON to be his Act and Deed and by the Court admitted to Record and is Recorded. Test JAS. LITTLEPAGE, Clk.

-This Indenture made the fifth day of August in the year of our Lord Christ one thousand seven hundred and fourty three Between EDWARD HARRIS of the parish of Fredricksville in Louisa County of the one part and WILLIAM HARRIS of the parish and County aforesaid of the other part. Witnesseth that the said EDWARD HARRIS for and in consideration of the sum of ten pounds current money of Virginia to him in hand paid by the said WILLIAM HARRIS the Receipt Whereof the said EDWARD HARRIS doth hereby acknowledge he the said EDWARD HARRIS have granted bargained and sold aliened & confirmed and by these presents do grant bargain and sell alien and confirm unto the said WILLIAM HARRIS his heirs and assigns for ever all the Tract or parcell of Land and plantation thereon situate lying and being in the parish of Fredricksville in the said County of Louisa containing by estimation fifty acres being the same more or less it being part of a greater tract whereon the said EDWARD HARRIS now liveth and bounded as followeth to wit beginning at Capt. DABNEY house north fifty degrees west twelve poles to a corner red oak saplin thence north seventy five degrees west fourteen poles thence north fifty five degrees west seventy five poles thence north seventy seven degrees west sixty two poles thence south fourty degrees west eighteen poles thence south fourty four and a half east one hundred and fifty five poles to the beginning and also all trees woods under woods Tiths Commons Common of pastures profits commodities advantages hereditaments waies waters and appurtenances whatsoever to the said fifty acres of Land and

p. Louisa County Deed Book A 12th September 1743
106 plantation above mentioned or in any wise appertaining and also the Reversion and Reversions Remainder and Remainders Rents and Services of the said premises and every part thereof and all the Estate Right Title Interest Claim and Demand whatsoever of him the said EDWARD HARRIS of in and to the said Tract of fifty acres of Land with the said plantation thereon and premises and every part thereof to have and to hold the said land and plantation and all and singular the premises above mentioned and every part thereof with the appurtenances unto the said WILLIAM HARRIS his heirs and assigns to the only proper use and behoof of the said WILLIAM HARRIS his heirs and assigns forever and the said EDWARD HARRIS for himself and his heirs the said Tract or parcel of fifty acres of Land and premises and every part thereof against himself and his heirs and all and every other person or persons whatsoever I the said EDWARD HARRIS have hereunto set my hand and seal the day and year first above written.

Signed Sealed and Delivered in presence of [blank] EDWARD HARRIS [seal]
Memorandum that on the 5th day of August 1743 peaceable and quiet possession was had and taken by the within named EDWARD HARRIS of the within granted land and premises and the same was by him delivered unto the within named WILLIAM HARRIS as the usual Symbol's of Livery and Seisen according to the force form and Effort of the within Deed in the presents of EDWARD HARRIS [seal]
5th of August 1743 Then Received the sum of ten pounds current money of Virginia it being the consideration money for the land and premises within granted Received the same of the within named WILLIAM HARRIS pd. me. Witness [blank]
At a Court held for Louisa County on Monday the 12th Sept. 1743.
This Indenture & Memorandum of Livery of Seisin and Receipt thereon endorsed was this day in open Court by EDWARD HARRIS acknowledged to be his Act and Deed & by the court admitted to Record and is Recorded. Test JAS. LITTLEPAGE, Clk.

p. Louisa County Deed Book A 12th September 1743
107 -This Indenture made the third day of August in the year of our Lord Christ one thousand seven hundred and fourty three Between WILLIAM HARRIS of Brunswick County of the one part and STEPHEN HARRIS of Saint Martin's Parish in Hanover of the other part Witnesseth that the said WILLIAM HARRIS for and in consideration of the sum of Twelve pounds XXXX current money of Virginia to him in Hand paid by the said STEPHEN HARRIS the receipt whereof he the said WILLIAM HARRIS do hereby acknowledge he the said WILLIAM HARRIS have granted bargained and sold aliened and confirmed and by these presents do

grant bargain and sell alien and confirm unto the said STEPHEN HARRIS his heirs and assigns forever all that Tract or parcell of land and plantation thereon situate lying and being in the parish of Fredricksville in the County of Louisa containing sixty two acres be the same more or less and bounded as followeth beginning at a corner of several marked white oake saplins runing north fourty five degrees east crossing Cub Creek to a corner white oake one hundred poles thence north thirty nine degrees west one hundred and pole to a corner pine and crosses Cub Creek again thence south fifty six degrees west seventy seven poles to a corner hickory saplin thence south twenty eight degrees east to the beginning and also all trees woods under woods Tiths commons common of pastures profits commodity's advantages heriditaments waies waters and appurtenances whatsoever to the said sixty two acres of land and plantation above mentioned Belonging or any wise appertaining and also the Reversion and Reversions Remainder and Remainders Rents and Services of the said premises and part thereof and all the Estate Right Title Interest Claim and demand whatsoever of him the said WILLIAM HARRIS of in and unto the said Tract or parcel of sixty two acres of Land with the said plantation thereon and premises and every part thereof to have and to hold the said Land and plantation and all and singular the premises above mentioned and every part and parcel thereof with the appurtenances unto the said STEPHEN HARRIS his heirs and assigns to the only use and behoof of the said STEPHEN HARRIS his heirs and assigns forever and the said WILLIAM HARRIS for himself and his heirs the said Tract or parcel of Sixty two acres of Land be the same more or less and premises and every part thereof against himself his heirs against all and every other person and persons whatsoever to the said STEPHEN HARRIS his heirs and assigns shall and will warrant and forever Defend by these presents In Witness whereof I the said WILLIAM HARRIS have hereunto

p. <u>Louisa County Deed Book A 12th September 1743</u>
108 set my hand and seal the day and year first above written.

Signed Sealed and Delivered WILLIAM HARRIS [seal]
in presence of us....

RICHARD HENDERSON, JAMES MOODY, JOHN X [his mark] ADAMS

Memorandum that the 3rd day of August 1743 peaceable and Quiet possession was had and taken by the within named WILLIAM HARRIS of the within granted Land and premises and the same was by him Delivered unto the within named STEPHEN HARRIS as the usual Symbol's of Livery of Seisin according to the force form & effort of the within Deed.

In the presents of WILLIAM HARRIS [seal]

Test RICHARD HENDERSON, JAMES MOODY, JOHN X [his mark] ADAMS

3 of August 1743 Then Received the sume of Twelve pounds current money of Virginia it being the consideration money for the Land & premises within granted Reced. the sume of the within named STEPHEN HARRIS pd. me.

Witness RICHARD HENDERSON, JAMES MOODY, JOHN X [his mark] ADAMS

At a Court held for Louisa County on Monday the 12th Sept. 1743.

This Indenture Memorandum of Livery of Seisin and Receipt thereon Endorsed was this day proved in open Court by the oaths of the Witnesses thereto to be the Act and Deed of WILLIAM HARRIS and by the Court was admitted to Record and is Recorded.

Test JAS. LITTLEPAGE, Clk.

-Know all men by these presents that I WILLIAM THOMASSON of the parish of Saint [blank] in the County of Louisa am held and stand firmly bound unto JOHN WORD of Saint Georges parish in the County of Spotsylvania in the full and just sume of two pounds four shillings curent money to be paid unto the said JOHN WORD his heirs Executors Administrators or assigns at upon the first day of December next for the payment whereof I bind in my heirs Executors Administrators to the said JOHN WORD his heirs or assigns under the penal sume

p. <u>Louisa County Deed Book A 12th September 1743</u>

109 of ten pounds eight shillings like curent money firmly by these presents and for the further security and more certain payment of the said sume unto the said JOHN WORD Know also that I have hereby sold assined conveyed made over and Transferd and I do by these sell assine make over bargain convey and Transfer unto the said JOHN WORD his heirs Executors Administrators or assines the following goods and chattels Vigiliet and small gray mair with a Long main and Taile and Branded on the Near buttock X and all her Increase and Likewise one three galland iron pot and one putor bason and one putor dish and two putor plaits to have and to hold the said Mair and other the premises to the said JOHN WORD his heirs or assines and as his proper goods and chattels forever provided allways and is the true Intent and Meaning of the said presents that if the said WILLIAM THOMASSON or any person in my behalf pay or Cause to be paid the aforesaid sume at the time aforesaid to the said JOHN WORD his heirs Executors Administrators or assines full power and Virtue In Witness whereof I have hereunto sett my hand and seal this twenty ninth day of August 1743. Sind Sealed and Delivered

In the presence of WILLIAM THOMASSON [seal]

GEORGE BRUCE, JOHN ALLEN

At a Court held for Louisa County the 12th day of Sept. 1743.

This Indenture was this day acknowledged in open Court by WILLIAM THOMASSON to be his Act and Deed and by the Court was admitted to Record and is Recorded.

Test JAS. LITTLEPAGE, Clk.

-This Indenture made this eleventh day of September in the year of our Lord Christ one thousand seven hundred and forty three Between CHAMPNESS TERRY of Louisa County planter of the one part and DANIEL WHITE of Orange County planter of the other part Witnesseth that the said CHAMPNESS TERRY for and in consideration of the sum of five shillings of good Lawfull money of England to him in hand paid by the said DANIEL WHITE, at and before the ensealing and Delivery of these presents the Receipt of which the said CHAMPNESS TERRY doth hereby own and acknowledge and from every part and parcel doth acquit Exonorate and Discharge the said DANIEL WHITE his heirs Executors Administrators and assigns have bargained and sold and do by these presents

p. Louisa County Deed Book A 12th September 1743
110 bargain sell and Make over Lease demise and farme Lett on unto the said DANIEL WHITE his heirs Executors, Admrs. & assignes one certain Tract or parcel of Land lying and situate in the County of Louisa on the Branches of Pamunky River containing three hundred acres and is bounded as followeth [Vizt.] Beginning at a pine corner to WILL BIBB by the side of a small branch runing thence south eighty four Degrees east one hundred and eighty two poles to a pine on the east side of a branch thence North thirty five degrees east three hundred and thirty eight poles to three pines corner to SYMS in a Vally thence North Eighty degrees west one hundred and eight poles to two pines on a Hills side thence south seventy eight degrees west to two pines on the west side of a branch thence south fifty seven degrees west forty six poles to a pine thence south thirteen degrees east twenty poles to a pine thence south five degrees west twenty eight poles to a pine thence south forty degrees west forty poles to a pine thence south forty poles to a pine thence south twenty degrees west fifty two poles to a pine thence south sixty eight degrees west fifty six poles thence south fifty five degrees west seventy six poles to a pine red oake and white oake on a stoop point in WILLIAM BIBBS line thence with his line south eleven degrees west thirty six poles to red oake saplin thence south twenty two degrees twenty two degrees east to the Beginning the aforesaid Messuage & tract of Land and premises with all Houses, Edifices and Buildings Gardens Orchards farms woods underwoods ways water courses prevelidges commoditys whatsoever to the said Land Belonging or in anywise appertaining and all and singular the Estate Right or Title whatsoever of him the said CHAMPNESS TERRY of in unto the said Land and every part and parcell thereof To Have and To Hold all and singular the said Messuage and Tract of Land and Every part and parcell thereof hereby bargained and sold Mentioned or Intended to be held in or hereby bargained and sold unto the DANIEL WHITE his heirs Exrs. Administrators and assigns from the day of the date hereof

p. Louisa County Deed Book A 12th September 1743
111 for during the term for the whole year from thence ensealing and fully complait & ended yielding and paying the aforesaid the yearly rent pepper corn the feast of St. Michael the Archangel only if the same be lawfully demanded to the intent that by these presents and of the statute for transferring uses into possession the said DANIEL WHITE may be in the actuale possession of the premises and be enabled to aueph of a grant of the reversion and inheritance have interchangeably their hands and seals the said month year above written. Signed Sealed and delivered

in presence of us CHAMPNESS TERRY [seal]

EDWARD WARD, JO. PULLIAM, W. BURRUS CHRISTIAN X [her mark] TERRY [seal]

At a Court held for Louisa County on Monday the XIIth day of September 1743.

JAS. LITTLEPAGE, Clk.

-This Indenture made this twelvth day of September in the year of our Lord Christ one thousand seven hundred and forty three Between CHAMPNESS TERRY & CHRISTIAN his wife of the County of Louisa planter of the one part and DANIEL WHITE of the County of Orange planter of the other part. Witnesseth that the said CHAMPNESS TERRY for and in consideration of the sum of thirty pounds current money of Virginia to the said CHAMPNESS TERRY in hand paid by the said DANIEL WHITE before the ensealing & delivery hereof of these presents the receipt whereof the said CHAMPNESS TERRY doth hereby acknowledge and himself therewith fully satisfied and paid and thereof and every part and parcell thereof do fully and absolutely acquit exonerate and discharge the said DANIEL WHITE his heirs Exrs. Admrs. assigns and every of them by these presents and of the sum of five shillings of Lawfull money of England to the said CHAMPNESS TERRY in hand paid by the said DANIEL WHITE the receipt whereof he doth likewise hereby acknowledge hath granted bargained sold released and confirmed by these presents doth freely clearly and absolutely grant bargain sell release and confirm unto the said DANIEL WHITE in his actual possession now being by the virtue of Bargain and sale to him thereof made for one whole year by Indenture bearing day before the date hereof & by force of the statute for transferring use into possession & unto his heirs & assigns all that messuage tract & parcell of Land lying being & situate in the County of Louisa on the branches of Pamunky river containing three hundred acres is bounded as followeth Vizt. Beginning at a pine corner to WILLIAM BIBB

p. <u>Louisa County Deed Book A 12th September 1743</u>

112 by the side of a small branch runing thence south eighty four Degrees east one hundred and eighty two poles to a pine on the east side of a branch thence North thirty five degrees east three hundred and thirty eight poles to three pines corner to SYMS in a Vally thence North Eighty degrees west one hundred and eight poles to two pines on a Hill side thence south seventy eight degrees west to two pines on the west side of a branch thence south fifty seven degrees west forty six poles to a pine thence south thirteen degrees east twenty poles to a pine thence south five degrees west twenty eight poles to a pine thence south forty degrees west forty poles to a pine thence south forty poles to a pine thence south twenty degrees west fifty two poles to a pine thence south sixty eight degrees west fifty six poles thence south fifty five degrees west seventy six poles to a pine red oake and white oake on a stoop point in WILLIAM BIBBS line thence with his line south eleven degrees west thirty six poles to red oake saplin thence south twenty two degrees twenty two degrees east to the Beginning the aforesaid Messuage & the said three hundred acres of Land being now in the tennure and occupation of the said CHAMPNESS TERRY and all singular the Houses, Orchards Gardens fences Meadows pastures feedings water water courses woods underwoods & all other hereditaments & appurtenances to the said granted premises belonging or in any ways appertaining & every part and parcell & the reversion reversions remainder & remainders yearly & other rents and profits and all the estate right title claim & demand whatsoever of him the said CHAMPNESS TERRY of in and into the said premises and whereof or wherein the said CHAMPNESS TERRY hath any Estate or Freehold or inheritance whatsoever of the premises & every part & parcell thereof To Have and To Hold the said messuage or plantation and the said three hundred acres of Land & all the

right title hereby granted bargained & sold revised released enfeoffed & confirmed and every part and parcell thereof with their & every of their appurtenances unto the said DANIEL WHITE to his heirs & assigns for or to the only proper use and behoof of the said DANIEL WHITE his heirs assignes for ever to be held on of the Lord or Lord of the fee or fees of the premises by the rents & services for the Land due to be paid And the said CHAMPNESS TERRY for himself his heirs Exrs. & Admrs. doth covenant to with the said DANIEL WHITE his heirs & assigns by these presents that the said CHAMPNESS TERRY now is and standeth lawfull & rightfully seised of the said three hundred acres of land with their appurtenances of a good sure perfect and indefeasable estate in fee simple and now hath good rightfull power and lawfull authority to grant & convey the said Land and premises unto the said DANIEL WHITE and his heirs and assignes according to the true intent meaning of these presents And that it shall and may be lawfull for the said DANIEL WHITE his heirs and assigns from

p. <u>Louisa County Deed Book A 12th September 1743</u>

113 time to time and at all times forever hereafter peaceably and quietly to have hold and possess and enjoy all the said three hundred acres of Land with their appurtenances without the lawfull Lot Suit or Trouble of him the said CHAMPNESS TERRY his heirs & assigns any other person or person lawfully claiming or to claim by from or under him them or any of them or any person or persons whatsoever and the said CHAMPNESS TERRY for himself his heirs Exrs. Admrs. and assignes shall and will at any time hereafter after the date hereof upon the reasonably request and at the costs & charges of the said DANIEL WHITE his heirs or assignes do make execute or cause to be done made or executed all & every such further act or acts conveyance or conveyances in the Law whatsoever for the further and better conveying & assuring the said three hundred acres of Land and premises with their appurtenances unto the said DANIEL WHITE his heirs & assignes forever as the Counsel Learned in the Law of the said DANIEL WHITE his heirs or assinges shall favorably devised or required to as the parties to make the same be not compelled to travill above fifty miles from the said premises for the doing the same and the said CHAMPNESS TERRY his heirs Exrs. Admrs. & assignes the said DANIEL WHITE his heirs & assignes shall hath rightfully & absolutely warrant and defend forever by these presents. Witness whereof the parties to these presents Indentures have interchangeably set their hands and seals the day and month & year above written.

Signed sealed and Delivered
in the presence of us the sum of thirty pounds current money being first paid

CHAMPNESS TERRY [seal]
CHRISTIAN X [her mark] TERRY [seal]

EDWARD WARD, JO. PULLIAM, W. BURRUS

At a Court held for Louisa County on Monday the XIIth day of September 1743.
This Indenture was this day in open court acknowledged by CHAMPNESS TERRY and CHRISTIAN his wife to be their Act & Deed the said CHRISTIAN being first privily examined as the Law Directs declaring her consent thereof thereupon it was by the Court admitted to record and is recorded. Test JAS. LITTLEPAGE, Clk.

-This Indenture made the fifteenth day of August in the year of our Lord Christ one thousand seven hundred and fourty three Between WILLIAM GOOCH of the parish of St. Martin's in the County of Hanover of the one part and BENJAMIN SPENCER of the aforesaid parish of St. Martin's in the County of Louisa of the other part. Witness that he the said WILLIAM GOOCH for and in consideration of the sume of ten pounds current money of Virginia to him in hand paid by the said BENJAMIN SPENCER his receipt whereof the said WILLIAM GOOCH do hereby acknowledge to the said WILLIAM GOOCH have granted bargained & sold aliened & confirmed and by these presents do grant bargain and sell alien and confirm unto the said BENJAMIN SPENCER his heirs & assignes forever and certain tract or parcell of Land situate lying and being in the parish of St. Martin in the County of Louisa bounded as followeth to with Beginning at a red oake in CHONIAS MAPLES line on the road thence along a line of marked trees to Col. JONES's pine thence along

p. Louisa County Deed Book A 12th September1743

114 a line of marked trees to RICHARD MULLINS's line, thence along the said MULLINS's line to the road thence along the said road side to MAPLES's red oak where it first begins continueth one hundred & eighty acres be the same more or less it being part of four hundred acres granted to DANIEL WILLIAM's by pattent bearing date the XXVIIth day of January in the year of our Lord MDCCXXXIV and also all trees woods underwoods tiths commons common of pastures profits commodities advantages hereditaments waies waters & appurtenances whatsoever to the said one hundred & eighty acres of Land above mentioned belonging or in any wise appertaining and also the Reversion & Reversions Remainder and Remainders rents & services of the said premises and of every part thereof and the estate right title claim & demand & all other interest whatsoever of him the said WILLIAM GOOCH of in & to the said tract or parcell of one hundred & eighty acres of Land and premises & every part thereof To Have and To Hold the said Land and all and singular the premises above mentioned & every part & parcell thereof with the appurtenances unto the said BENJAMIN SPENCER his heirs & assignes to the only proper use & behoof of the said BENJAMIN SPENCER his heirs & assignes forever and the said WILLIAM GOOCH for himself & his heirs the said tract or parcell of one hundred eighty acres of land be the same more or less & premises & every part thereof against himself & his heirs & against all & every other person or persons whatsoever to the said BENJAMIN SPENCER his heirs & assignes shall will warrant and forever defend by these presents. In Witness whereof the said WILLIAM GOOCH to these presents have set my hand and affixed my seal the day & year first above written.

Signed Sealed and Delivered Signing
in presence of us ROBT. SHARP WILLIAM W GOOCH [seal]

Memorandum that on the XVth day of August MDCCXXXXIII peaceable & quiet possession was had & taken by the within named WILLIAM GOOCH of the within granted land and premises and the same was by him delivered unto the within named BENJAMIN SPENCER as the usual Symbols of livery of seisin according to the force form & effort of the within Deed in the presence of us ROBERT SHARP Signing WILLIAM W GOOCH [[seal]

XVth of August MDCCXXXXIII then received the sum of ten pounds current money of Virginia it being the consideration money for the lands and premises within granted received the sume of the within named BENJAMIN SPENCER by us.

Witness ROBERT SHARP Signing WILLIAM W GOOCH

At a Court held for Louisa County on Monday the 12th day of September.

This Indenture & Memorandum of livery of seisin & receipt was this day in open Court acknowledged by WILLIAM GOOCH to be his Act and Deed & by the Court admitted to record & is recorded. Test JAS. LITTLEPAGE, Clk. Truly Recorded

p. Louisa County Deed Book A 12th September 1743

115 This day also ELIZABETH the wife of the said WILLIAM GOOCH being first privily examined as the Law directs & declaring her consent thereto did in open Court relinquish unto the said BENJAMIN SPENCER the right of dower which she hath in the land conveyed by the said Indenture & the same by the Court was admitted to record & is recorded. Test JAS. LITTLEPAGE, Clk.

-This Indenture made this twelfth day of September in the year of our Lord Christ one thousand seven hundred and fourty three Between WILLIAM WINSTON, JUN. of the parish of St. Martin in the County of Hanover & SARAH his wife of the one part and JOHN WINSTON of the parish of St. Paul and County aforesaid of the other part. Witnesseth that the said WILLIAM WINSTON for and in consideration of fifty five pounds current money to him in hand paid before sealing of and delivery of these presents the receipt whereof he doth hereby acknowledge and himself therewith fully satisfied contented and paid & thereof & of every part & parcell thereof doth hereby acquit & discharge the said JOHN WINSTON his heirs Exrs. Admrs. & forever Hath granted sold aliened enfeoffed and confirmed and by these presents doth grant and sell alien confirm enfeoff & confirm unto the said JOHN WINSTON his heirs & assignes forever and certain tract or parcell of land situate lying and being in the parish of Fredericksville in the County of Louisa by estimation five hundred & fifty acres be the same more or less according to the bounded thereof Vizt. beginning at a corner pine in THOMAS RICES line runing thence south twenty west three hundred & thirty six poles to his & Col. WILLIAM MERIWETHER's corner pine thence along MERIWETHER's line north fourty two west three hundred & twelve poles to a pine and black oak saplin in the said line thence north fifty four and half east three hundred and twenty eight poles to the beginning To Have and To Hold and peaceably to enjoy the said five hundred & fifty acres of Land above bounded with all houses orchards gardens woods ways waters underwoods and meadows with all other & singular the hereditaments and appurtenances thereto belonging or in any wise appertaining from the claim right or title of them the said WILLIAM WINSTON & SARAH his wife his heirs Exrs. or any other person or persons whatsoever to the only proper use and behoof of him the said JOHN WINSTON his heirs Exrs. & assignes forever & to no other use intent or purpose whatsoever and the said WILLIAM WINSTON for himself his heirs Exs. doth covenant promise & agree that he will from time to time & at all times hereafter against all persons whatsoever the above said five hundred & fifty acres of land and premises warrant

& forever defend to the said JOHN WINSTON his heirs & assignes to the said WILLIAM WINSTON & SARAH his wife for themselves their heirs Exrs. &c. further that they & their heirs will at any time forever hereafter make any further right conveyance or like that he the said JOHN WINSTON his heirs or assignes or his or their council learned in the Law shall devise or require and acknowledge the same in open Court when they shall be thereunto Lawfully required. In Witness whereof the said WILLIAM WINSTON & SARAH his wife have hereunto set their hands and seals the day & year first above written.

Signed Sealed and delivered in the presence of

WILLIAM WINSTON, JUN. [seal]
SARAH WINSTON [seal]

p. Louisa County Deed Book A 12th September 1743

116 received of the within named JOHN WINSTON the sum of fifty five pounds current money being the consideration for the Land & premises within mentioned As Witness my hand this 12th day of September 1743.

Test JOHN CARR, CHS. BARRET WILLIAM WINSTON, JUN.

At a Court held for Louisa County on Monday the 12th day of September 1743.
This Indenture & receipt were this day in open Court acknowledged by WILLIAM WINSTON, JUN. & SARAH his wife to be their Act & deed the said SARAH being first privily examined as the Law directs & declaring her consent thereto & thereupon it was by the Court admitted to record & is recorded. Test JAS. LITTLEPAGE, Clk. Truly Recorded

-This Indenture made this tenth day of October in the year of our Lord God one thousand seven hundred and forty three Between THOMAS RICE of St. Martin's parish of the County of Hanover of one part & JOHN WADKINS of Louisa County of the parish of Fredericksville of the other part. Witnesseth that the said THOMAS RICE for and in consideration of the sum of ten pounds Sterling to him in hand paid by the said JOHN WADKINS before the sealing & delivery of these presents the receipt whereof he the said THOMAS RICE doth hereby acknowledge and thereof doth clearly acquit and discharge the said JOHN WADKINS his heirs & assignes by these presents hath granted bargained sold and enfeoffed & confirmed and by these presents doth grant bargain and sell enfeoff and confirm unto the said JOHN WADKINS and certain tract or parcell of land containing seventy five acres lying and being the south side of the main fork of Cub Creek near the head in the County & parish aforesaid & bounded as followeth to wit Beginning at BENNET's corner red oak standing in the Low grounds of Cub Creek thence along CRENSHAW's line to his corner of one pine and white oake thence along RICE's line crossing Cattalo Craick to WINSTON's corner of saplin thence along WINSTON's line to Cub Creek thence down the road keeping the way or courses to [unreadable] the place where it first began To Have and To Hold the said tract or land containing seventy five acres be the same more or less together with all houses & appurtenances thereunto belonging & appertaining unto the said JOHN WADKINS his heirs & assignes forever more free & clear from all or any claim title or demand of him the said THOMAS RICE his heirs and of all or any other person or persons whatsoever claiming by from or under him them or any of them and he the said THOMAS RICE for himself his heirs &c. doth covenant promise agree to and with the said JOHN WADKINS his heirs &c. that he the said THOMAS RICE his heirs &c. shall will at any time or times hereafter when thereunto required by the said JOHN WADKINS his heirs &c. make such further & other conveyances for the better transferring & assuring the said Land unto the said JOHN WADKINS his heirs & assigns in such manner & by such deed as he the said JOHN WADKINS his heirs & assignes they or any of them shall at any time hereafter at the cost & charge of

p. Louisa County Deed Book A 10th October 1743

117 the said JOHN WADKINS his heirs &c. require & also that he the said THOMAS RICE his heirs &c. all the land and premises aforesaid with the appurtenances will warrant and forever defend by these presents unto him the said JOHN WADKINS his heirs & assignes against him the said THOMAS RICE his heirs &c. and against all & every other person or persons whatsoever. In Witness whereof the said THOMAS RICE hath hereunto set his hand & seal the day and year above written.

Signed Sealed & delivered in presence of THOMAS RICE [seal]

RICHARD PICKERING, THOMAS LANKFORD, JAMES MILLES

Memorandum that on this fourth day of October one thousand seven hundred & forty three I THOMAS RICE do acknowledge to have made Livery of Seizen of the Land and premises in the within deed contained by the delivery of Turf and Twigg of the said Land unto the said JOHN WADKINS his heirs & assignes forever according to the force of form of the within deed as Witness my hand & seal the day & year above written.

JAMES MILLES, THOMAS LANKFORD, RICHARD PICKERING THOMAS RICE [seal]

At a Court held for Louisa County on Monday the 10th day of October 1743.
This Indenture & Memorandum of Livery of Seisen was this day in open Court acknowledged by THOMAS RICE to be his act and deed and by the Court admitted to record & is recorded.

Test JAS. LITTLEPAGE, Clk. Truly Recorded JAS. LITTLEPAGE

-This Indenture made this tenth day of October in the year of our Lord Sovereign King George the second by the Grace of God of Great Britain France and Ireland King Defender of the faith &c. and in the year of our Lord MDCCXLIII Between THOMAS WINGFIELD of the County of Hanover and SARAH his wife of the one part and JAMES WINSTON of the said County of the other part. Witnesseth that the said THOMAS WINGFIELD & SARAH his wife for and in consideration of the sum of forty five pounds current money of Virginia to him in hand paid by the said JAMES WINGFIELD at and before the ensealing and delivery of these presents the receipt whereof he the said THOMAS WINGFIELD & SARAH his wife doth hereby acknowledge have & each of them hath granted bargained sold, aliened and confirmed & by these presents doth grant bargain and sell alien enfeoff and confirm unto the said JAMES WINSTON all that tract or parcel of land situate lying and being between the north fork of Elk Creek and contrary in the parish of Fredrixville and County of Louisa containing eight hundred acres [more or less] it being part of a parcel granted to JOHN POINDEXTER & by him conveyed to the said THOMAS WINGFIELD by deed in Hanover County Court and is bounded as followeth, to wit, Beginning at

p. <u>Louisa County Deed Book A 10th October 1743</u>

118 BARBARY WINSTONS & W. POWELS corner four pines and a black oak runing along POWELS lines south fifty five west one hundred and ninety four poles to several marked trees south to only six west sixteen poles to two red oaks thence north eighty four west two hundred & thirty four poles to the said POWELS corner by a slash thence continued the course north eighty four west ninety eight poles to a red oak by a vally thence north six east one hundred and forty six poles to five marked trees in BENJAMIN BROWN's line thence along the same north forty five east one hundred and fifty five poles to a red oak and pine thence south forty four east one hundred and fourteen poles to a red oak thence north forty four east three hundred & fifteen poles to a srubby white oak saplin in Mr. CHISWELL's line, thence along the same south sixty four west two hundred and fifty eight poles to two red oaks by a glade of Elk Creek in BARBARY WINSTON's line, thence along the same south fifty five west three hundred & twenty poles to the beginning with all houses edifices gardens orchards woods underwoods pastures feedings & profits to the said Land belonging in any wise appertaining and the Reversion & Reversions Remainder & Remainders thereof and all the right title claim and demand of him the said THOMAS WINGFIELD & SARAH his wife in or to the said Land and premises & every part To Have and To Hold the said tract or parcel of land containing eight hundred acres aforesaid & all & singular other the premises with their & every of their appurtenances unto the said JAMES WINSTON his heirs and assigns forever to the only proper use and behoof of him the said JAMES WINSTON for his heirs & assigns forever and the said THOMAS WINGFILED & SARAH his wife to covenant & agree to & with the said JAMES WINSTON his heirs Exrs. Admrs. & assigns in manner following that the said JAMES WINSTON his heirs and assigns shall & may from time to time & at all times hereafter Quietly and peaceably have hold possess & enjoy the above Granted Land and premises and every part thereof with the appurtenances without any Lawful lot suit Trouble or eviction or Molestation of him the said THOMAS WINGFIELD and SARAH his wife their heirs or assigns or of any other person or persons whatsoever claiming or to claim by from or under him them or any of them & that free & clear and freely & clearly aquitted and discharged or by the said THOMAS WINGFIELD his heirs Exors. & Admors. or some of them from time to time and at all times hereafter kept hereafter and from all and all manner of former or other bargains sails gifts grants intails dowers and title of dowers & all other charges and Incumbrances whatsoever had made committed done or suffered by him the said THOMAS WINGFIELD the said Land and premises herein before bargained and sold with there and every of there appurtenances unto the said JAMES WINSTON his heirs and assigns shall and will warrant and for ever defend by these presents. In Witness whereof the parties to these presents their hands and seals have sett the day & year first above written.

Signed Sealed & Delivered in presence of
NATH. JOUET, JO. FOX, JO. WILLIAMS

[Interlined before signed in the eighteenth line from the top this word {arros}]

THOMAS WINGFIELD [seal]
SARAH WINGFIELD [seal]

At a Court held for Louisa County on Monday the tenth day of October 1743.

This Indenture was this day in open Court acknowledged by THOMAS WINGFIELD to be his act and deed & by the Court ordered to be recorded. Test JAS. LITTLEPAGE, Clk. Acknowledged before us at the house of the within named THOMAS WINGFIELD

p. Louisa County Deed Book A 10th October 1743
119 by the said SARAH WINGFIELD the fifth day of Nov. 1743 she being first privily and apart examined by us THO. COLLER and JAMES OVERTON

-George the Second by the Grace of God of Great Britain France and Ireland King defender of the faith &c. To THOMAS COLLER, JAMES OVERTON & JOHN CHISWELL, Gent. Justices of Hanover County Greeting: Whereas THOMAS WINGFIELD of the County of Hanover and SARAH his wife have agreed to assure and convey to JAMES WINSTON of the said County in fee simple estate of and in all that tract or parcell of land situate lying and being between the north fork of Elk Creek in the parish of Fredericksville and County of Louisa containing eight hundred acres more or less it being part of a patent Granted to JOHN POINDEXTER & by him conveyed to the said THOMAS WINGFIELD with the appurtenances in the parish aforesaid by such sufficient deed or deeds in writing as by the said JAMES WINSTON or his Council Learned in the Law shall be advised and required and the said SARAH is informing that without Great danger of her body she cannot travell to the Court of our said County of Louisa there to make such acknowledgment as in that case is required as we have received We the state of the said SARAH commiserating in this case Have given you power to take the acknowledgment which the said SARAH shall be willing to make to you concerning the premises Therefore We command you that personally repairing to the said SARAH you take her acknowledgment aforesaid and when you shall have taken it that you return the same under your seals to our Justices at the Court thereof our said County of Louisa that the same together with such deed or deeds may be recorded sending to the same Justices this writ. Witness JAMES LITTLEPAGE Clerk of our said Court dated this XIII day of October 1743. JAMES LITTLEPAGE, Clk. Cur.
By virtue of this writ to us directed we have privily and a part examined the within named SARAH WINGFIELD wife to the within named THOMAS WINGFIELD who declared that she acknowledged all her right and title to the within mentioned Land and premises and that she did it freely without any force or compulsion witness our hands and seals this fifth day of November 1743. THOMAS COLLER [seal] JAMES OVERTON [seal]
At a Court held for Louisa County on Monday the XIIth day of December 1743.
This Commission with certificates therein written being presented here in court and ordered to be recorded. JAS. LITTLEPAGE, Clerk

-This Indenture made this sixth day of October in the year of our Lord Christ one thousand seven hundred and forty three Between ZACHARIAH COLLIER of the parish of Saint Paul in the County of Louisa of the one part and WILLIAM VICTORY of St. John's parish in the County of King William of the other part. Witness that the said ZACHARIAH COLLIER for & in consideration of the sum of twenty pounds current money of Virginia to him paid by the said

WILLIAM VICTORY at and before the ensealing and delivery of these presents the receipt whereof he doth hereby acknowledge and thereof and of every part and parcell of the same doth hereby acquit and discharge the said WILLIAM VICTORY his Executors and Administrators and every of them by these presents hath granted aliened released enfeoffed and confirmed and by these presents for the consideration above set down doth grant alien release enfeoff and confirm unto the said WILLIAM VICTORY his heirs and assigns forever all that the said ZACHARIAH COLLIER his parcell or tract of land containing three hundred and fifty acres lying on the branches of Golden Mine Creek in the aforesaid County of Louisa and is bounded as followeth, to wit, beginning at RICHARD CARTERs corner forked line in W. JOUETs line runing thereon

p. Louisa County Deed Book A 12th December 1743

120 the same north sixty four degrees west two hundred seventy eight poles to his and Colonel MERIWETHER's corner several pines thence on MERIWETHER's line north fifty eight poles to ELLIS HUGHES corner white oak and two pines in MERIWETHER;s line thence on HUGHES line east one hundred seventy four poles to a white oak and two hickory bushes and north six degrees east four hundred poles to HUGHES corner three pines thence east fourteen poles to several pines in Mr. AYLET's line thence along the said AYLET's line south five degrees west two hundred fifty two poles to a white oak and south eighty five degrees east one hundred & twenty four poles to RICHARD CARTER's corner stake between pointers of pines in AYLET's line thence on CARTER's line south fifteen degrees thirty nine west three hundred & thirty poles to the first stake on which said three hundred and fifty two acres of land above bounded is part of a patent for four hundred and sixteen acres and one whole patent for one hundred and eighty six acres both granted to the said ZACHARIAH COLLIER and all the estate right title interest into property claim and demand whatsoever of him the said ZACHARIAH COLLIER his heirs & assigns of in or unto the premises & the reversion & reversions remainder and remainders yearly & other rents & profits of the premises and of every part and parcell thereof To Have and To Hold the said three hundred and fifty two acres of land above bounded & all and singular other the premises with their and every of their appurtenances unto the said WILLIAM VICTORY and his heirs to the only use of the said WILLIAM VICTORY and of his heirs & assigns forever and the said ZACHARIAH COLLIER for himself his heirs Exrs. & Admrs. doth covenant and grant to and with the said WILLIAM VICTORY his heirs and assigns by these presents that the said ZACHARIAH COLLIER now is and standeth lawfully and rightfully seised of an in the said three hundred and fifty acres of land above bounded of a good such perfect absolute and indefesiable estate in fee simple and now hath good rightfull power and lawfull and absolute authority to grant and convey the same according to the purport true intent and meaning of these presents and shall and may be lawfull to and for the said WILLIAM VICTORY his heirs and assigns from time to time and at all times forever hereafter peaceably and quietly to have hold occupy possess use and enjoy the said three hundred and fifty two acres of land above bounded with their & every of their appurtenances without the lawfull lot suite trouble eviction or Molestation of him the said ZACHARIAH COLLIER his heirs or assigns or any other person or

persons whatsoever discharged of and from all future branches or evictions whatsoever the Quitrents from hence forth to our Sovereign Lord the King his heirs and Successors only excepted and foreprized and the said ZACHARIAH COLLIER and his heirs and all claiming or to claim right in by from or under him them or any of them or any other person or persons whatsoever shall and will warrant and forever defend by these presents. In Testimony of all which the said ZACHARIAH COLLIER to those presents tract interchangeably set his hand and affixed his seal the day and year first above written.

Signed sealed and delivered in the presence of us

JOHN CARR, JOHN SKARRAFF, DAVID ROACH ZACHARIAH COLLIER [seal]

Memorandum that peaceable and quiet possession of the within mentioned presents was first had and taken by the within named ZACHARIAH COLLIER and by him delivered to the within named WILLIAM VICTORY by the delivery of Turf and

p. <u>Louisa County Deed Book A 12th December 1743</u>

121 Twigg of the Ground of the said Land as the usual Symbols of livery of seisen to do by him hold according to the within Indenture.

Inn the presence of ZACHARIAH COLLIER

Received of the within named WILLIAM VICTORY the sum of twenty pounds current money of Virginia being the consideration within mentioned witness my hand the sixty day of October one thousand seven hundred and forty three.

Witness JOHN CARR ZACHARIAH COLLIER

JOHN SKARRAFF, DAVID ROACH

At a Court held for Louisa County on Monday the 10th day of October 1743.
This Indenture & Memorandum of livery of seisen & receipt was this day in open court proved to be the act & deed of the said ZACHARIAH COLLIER by the oaths of JOHN SKARRAFF & DAVID ROACH two of the witnesses thereto.Test JAMES LITTLEPAGE, Clk, Cur.

-This Indenture made this eighth day of October in the year of our Lord Christ one thousand seven hundred and forty three Between ZACHARIAH COLLIER of the parish of Saint Martin in the County of Louisa of the one part and RICHARD CARTER of the parish of Fredericksville in the aforesaid County of the other part. Witnesseth that the said ZACHARIAH COLLIER for and in consideration of the sum of twelve pounds current money of Virginia to him in hand paid be the said RICHARD CARTER at and before the ensealing and delivery of these presents the receipt whereof he doth hereby acknowledge & thereof and of every part and parcel thereof doth clearly acquit & discharge the said RICHARD CARTER his Executors and Administrators to them by these presents hath granted aliened released enfeoffed and confirmed by these presents for the consideration above set down doth grant alien release enfeoff and confirm unto the said RICHARD CARTER & to his heirs and assigns forever all that the said ZACHARIAH COLLIER his parcel or tract of land containing two hundred and fifty acres lying on the branches of Golden Myne Creek in the aforesaid parish of Fredericksville & county of Louisa Bounded as followeth to wit Beginning at THOMAS ADAMS corner state between two pines in Mr. AYLETT's line runing thence on ADAMS's line south two degrees west three hundred eighty three poles to a pine and white oak in Mr. JOUET's line thence along the same north sixty four degrees west one hundred sixty one poles to aforesaid pine in the said line thence north sixteen degrees thirty minutes east three hundred & thirty poles to a stake between pointer's of pines in Mr. AYLET's line, thence along the same south eighty five east seventy poles to the beginning which said two hundred and fifty acres above bounded is part of a Greater tract granted by patent to the said ZACHARIAH COLLIER and all the estate Right Title interest use property claim and demand whatsoever of him the said ZACHARIAH COLLIER of in or unto the premises and the Reversion and Reversions Remainder and Remainders yearly and other rents & profits of the premises and of every part and parcel thereof To Have and to Hold the said two hundred and fifty acres of land above bounded & all & singular other the premises herein before mentioned & intended to be hereby granted with their and every of their appurtenances unto the said RICHARD CARTER & his heirs to the only use and behoof of the said RICHARD CARTER & of his heirs and assigns forever, and the said ZACHARIAH COLLIER for himself his heirs Exrs. and Admors. doth covenant and Grant to and with the said RICHARD CARTER his heirs & assigns by these presents that he the said ZACHARIAH COLLIER now is and standeth lawfully & rightfully seised of & in the said two hundred and fifty acres of land above bounded of a Good sure perfect absolute

p. Louisa County Deed Book A 12th December 1743

122 and indefeasable estate in fee simple and now hath good right full power & lawfull and absolute authority to grant and convey the same according to the purport true intent and meaning of these presents and that it shall and may be lawfull to and for the said RICHARD CARTER his heirs and assigns from time to time and at all times forever hereafter peaceably and quietly to have hold occupy possess use and enjoy the said two hundred and fifty acres of land above bounded without any lawful lott suit trouble or interruption of him the said ZACHARIAH COLLIER his heirs or assigns or any other person or persons whatsoever discharged of and from all Incumbrances or Evictions whatsoever the Quitrents from hence forth to Grow due to our Sovereign Lord the King his heirs and Successors only excepted and foreprized and the said ZACHARIAH COLLIER for himself his heirs Executors and Administrators the aforesaid Granted premises with their appurtenances unto the said RICHARD CARTER and his heirs against him the said ZACHARIAH COLLIER and his heirs and assigns claiming or to claim Right in by from or under him them or any of them or any of them or any other person or persons whatsoever shall and will warrant forever and defend by these presents. In Witness whereof the said ZACHARIAH COLLIER to these presents shall interchangeably set his hand and affixed his seal the day and year first above written.

Sealed and Delivered in presence of

JOHN CARR, WILLIAM OVERTON, JAMES WINSTON ZACHARIAH COLLIER [seal]

Memorandum that peaceable and quiet possession of the within mentioned premises was first had and taken by the within named ZACHARIAH COLLIER and by him delivered to the within named RICHARD CARTER by the delivery of Turf and Twigg of the Ground of the said Land as the usual Symbols of livery of seisen to be by him held according to the within

written Indenture. in the presence of
JOHN CARR, WILLIAM OVERTON, JAMES WINSTON ZACHARIAH COLLIER
Dec. 12 1743 Then Received the within consideration of twelve pounds of RICHARD CARTER I say noted. Test RICHARD PICKERING Pr. ZACHARIAH COLLIER
At a Court held for Louisa County on Monday the 12th day of December 1743.
This Indenture & Memorandum of livery of seisen & receipt was this day in open court acknowledged by ZACHARIAH COLLIER to be his act & deed by the Court ordered to be recorded. Test THOMAS PERKINS Pr. JAS. LITTLEPAGE, Clk.

-This Indenture made the twelfth day of December in the year of our Lord Christ one thousand seven hundred and forty three Between JOHN BLALOCK the older of the parish of Fredericksville in the County of Louisa of the one part and DANIEL BURFORD the older of the parish of Saint John in the County of King William of the other part Witnesseth that the said JOHN BLALOCK for and in consideration of the sum of thirty two pounds twelve shillings & ten pence current money of Virginia to him in hand paid by the said DANIEL BURFORD the receipt whereof he doth hereby acknowledge hath granted bargained and sold aliened and confirmed and by these presents doth grant bargain and sell alien and confirm

p. <u>Louisa County Deed Book A 12th December 1743</u>
123 unto the said DANIEL BURFORD his heirs and assigns forever All that tract or parcel of land containing by estimation two hundred and fifty two acres be the same more or less situate lying and being in the parish of Fredericksville in the County of Louisa aforesaid and is bounded as followeth Beginning at the lower branch of Cub Creek at the bridge in BLALOCK's Road thence down the run of the said branch thence along THOMAS HARRIS's line north fifty three degrees & an half west sixty nine poles to a corner pine by the said BLALOCK's fence thence along another of the said HARRIS's lines south seventy three degrees west thirty two poles and an half to another corner pine thence along another of the said HARRIS's north forty seven degrees west ninety two poles to another corner pine marked with the Letter R thence along PHILIP TIMBERLAKE's line north thirty one degrees east to a corner white oak on the north side of BLALOCK's roast marked with the letters BR being a corner between the said TIMBERLAKE and WILLIAM BLALOCK thence the same course along WILLIAM BLALOCK's line to a corner pine by another pine marked with the Letter W two hundred and thirty five poles thence along Mr. JOSEPH GOOCH line south forty one east to a small white oak corner one hundred and seventy two poles thence along the line of the Land belonging to JOHN ANDERSON by the said JOHN BLALOCK now lives part thereof being part of four hundred acres granted to THOMAS POINDEXTER by patent bearing date the twenty fourth day of March one thousand seven hundred and twenty five and the other part thereof being part of one thousand and twenty acres granted to the said JOHN BLALOCK by patent bearing date the twentyeth day of June one thousand seven hundred and thirty three and all houses buildings fences orchards trees woods underwoods comodities & moluments profits and appurtenances whatsoever to the said tract or parcel of land belonging or in any wise appertaining or therewith usually occupied used or enjoyed or

reputed taken or known to be part or member thereof And the reversion and reversions Remainder and Remainders issues and profits thereof and of every part thereof and all the estate right title and property claim and demand whatsoever of the said JOHN BLALOCK his heirs and assigns of in and to the same or any part thereof To Have and To Hold the said tract or parcel of land & all and singular the premises herein before mentioned or intended to be hereby granted bargained & sold with their and every of their appurtenances to the said DANIEL BURFORD his heirs and assigns to the only use and behoof of him the said DANIEL BURFORD his heirs and assigns forever and the said JOHN BLALOCK for himself his heirs Exors. and Admors. doth covenant promise grant and agree to and with the said DANIEL BURFORD his heirs & assigns by these presents in manner and form following that is to say that he the said JOHN BLALOCK now is and stands lawfully seized of a good sure perfect absolute and indefeasible estate in fee simple in the premises and hath good right to sell and convey the same in manner and form aforesaid and that the said DANIEL BURFORD his heirs and assigns shall and may forever hereafter peaceable and quietly have hold occupy or discharge of him the said JOHN BLALOCK his heirs or assigns or any other person or persons whatsoever having or lawfully claiming any right or title thereon or thereto and that free and discharged of and from all former & other estates Rights & Titles and of and from all Judgments and Exenitions debts Mortgages & other Incumbrances whatsoever and that the said JOHN BLALOCK and his heirs and all and every other person or persons lawfully claiming any estate right title or interest of in or into the premises or any part or parcel thereof by from or under the said

p. <u>Louisa County Deed Book A 12th December 1743</u>

124 JOHN BLALOCK his heirs or assigns or otherwise shall and will at all times hereafter upon the reasonable request and at the costs and charges in the Law of the said DANIEL BURFORD his heirs and assigns make do perform acknowledge levy and execute or suffer or cause to be made done performed acknowledged levyed and exenited and suffered all and every such further & other Lawfull and reasonable act and acts thing and things device and devices assurance and assurances conveyance and conveyances in the Law whatsoever for the further better and more perfect assuring sure making and conveying the said land and assigns forever as by the said DANIEL BURFORD or by his or their councel learned in the law shall be reasonable devised advised or required and the said JOHN BLALOCK and his heirs all & singular the premises with the appurtenances unto the said DANIEL BURFORD his heirs and assigns shall and will warrant and forever defend by these presents. In Witness whereof the said parties to these presents have interchangeably set their hands and seals the day and year first above written.

Sealed & Delivered in presence of

JO. BICKLEY, JNO. PRYOR, BENJAMIN HENSON, JOHN CARR, JEREMIAH GLEN, WM. BURFORD

JOHN BLALOCK [seal]

Received the day and year first within mentioned of the within named DANIEL BURFORD the sum of thirty two pounds twelve shillings & ten pence current money being the consideration money within mentioned.

JO. BICKLEY, JNO. PRYOR, BENJAMIN HENSON, JOHN BLALOCK
JOHN CARR, JEREMIAH GLEN, WM. BURFORD

At a Court held for Louisa County on Monday the 12th day of December 1743.
This Indenture and receipt was this day in open Court acknowledged by JOHN BLALOCK to be his act & deed & by the Court admitted to record and is recorded.
Test JAMES LITTLEPAGE, Clk. Cur.

-Know all men by these presents that JOHN BLALOCK of the parish of Fredericksville in the County of Louisa am held and firmly bound unto the said DANIEL BURFORD of the parish of St. John in the County of King William in the full sum of fifty five pounds five shillings and eight pence current money to the which payment well & truly to be made to the said DANIEL BURFORD his heirs or assigns I bind my self my heirs Exors. and Admors. firmly by these presents sealed with my seal and dated this twelfth day of December Anno q Dom 1743.

p. Louisa County Deed Book A 12th December 1743

125 -The Condition of this obligation is such that if the above bounded JOHN BLALOCK his heirs Exors. and Admors. shall and do well & truly observe and perform fullfill accomplish and keep all and singular the covenants grants clauses and agreements comprized and mentioned in and Indenture of Bargain and Sale made between the said JOHN BLALOCK of the one part and the said DANIEL BURFORD of the other part bearing even date with these presents which on his and their parts are or ought to be performed fullfilled accomplished and kept according to the purport true intent and meaning of the same Indenture then this obligation to be void otherwise to stand and remain in full force & virtue. Sealed & Delivered in presence of

JO. BICKLEY, JNO. PRYOR, BENJAMIN HENSON, JOHN BLALOCK [seal]
JOHN CARR, JEREMIAH GLEN, WM. BURFORD

At a Court held for Louisa County on Monday the 12th day of December 1743.
This Bond was this day in open Court acknowledged by JOHN BLALOCK to be his act & deed and by the Court admitted to record and is recorded. Test JAMES LITTLEPAGE, Clk. Cur.

-In Pursuant to another order of Court we the Subscribers being first sworn before the Majestrate of this County, have valued the improvements on four hundred acres of land lying on the North fork of Moremans River in this County belonging to JOHN STARKE.

Vizt. To going to Williamsburg for the patent....................£1.10.0
To building a house....................£13.10.0
To building a Camp diging alrosh and falling trees....................£2.10.0
To one Negro Man....................£45.0.0
To two horses....................£29.0.0
To planting of peach trees....................£1.5.0
JOSEPH KEALLAN, JOHN DICKENSON....................£93.5.0

At a Court held for Louisa County on Monday the 9th day of January 1744.

This amount of the valuation of the improvements made on the Land of JOHN STARKE being this day returned in Court is ordered to be recorded and the said JOHN STARKE made oath that the said improvements have never before been valued to save any land that he know of.

-This Indenture made this eleventh day of February in the year of our Lord Christ one thousand seven hundred and forty three Between BENJAMIN HENSLEY of Louisa County of the one part and JOHN HENSLEY of the aforesaid County of the other part. Witnesseth that the said BENJAMIN HENSLEY for and in consideration of the sum of ten pounds current money of Virginia to him in hand paid by the said JOHN HENSLEY at and before the ensealing and delivery of these presents the receipt whereof he doth hereby acknowledge and thereof and of every part and parcell of the same doth hereby acquit and discharge the said JOHN HENSLEY his Exrs. and Admrs. and every of them by these presents hath granted aliened released enfeoffed and confirmed and by these presents for the consideration above set down doth grant alien released enfeoffe and perpetually confirm unto the said JOHN HENSLEY and to his heirs and assigns forever All that one hundred acres of Land situate and being on the North side of Wolf Swamp in the aforesaid County and is bounded

p. <u>Louisa County Deed Book A 13th February 1744</u>

126 as followeth to wit beginning at MILDRED MERIWETHER's corner stake runing thence south fifty east ten poles to a double horn beam on he north side of Wolf Trap Swamp thence up the said Swamp twenty poles to the Mouth of the south fork thereof thence up the said south fork by the meanders in a Right line forty five poles to two Spanish oakes and a white oak on the said south fork, thence south nine degrees thirty minites east one hundred and fifty poles to a hiccory saplin in SAMUEL BROCKMAN's line, thence on the same south forty four west forty four poles to him and RICHARD HAMMOCKS corner thence on HAMMOCKS line 4 north fifty six degrees thirty minutes east one hundred foreteen poles to MERIWETHER's corner two pines in the said line, thence on MERIWETHER's line north foreteen east one hundred and twenty nine poles to the beginning, And all the estate right Interest use property ad claim of him the said BENJAMIN HENSLEY of in or unto the premises and the Reversion and Reversions Remainder and Remainders yearly & other rents and profits of the premises and of every part & parcell thereof To Have and To Hold the said one hundred acres of Land above bounded and all and singular other the premises herein before Mentioned and Intended to be hereby Granted with their appurtenances unto the said JOHN HENSLEY and his heirs to the only use & behoof of him the said JOHN HENSLEY and of his heirs and assigns forever, and the said BENJAMIN HENSLEY for himself his heirs Exrs. and Admrs. doth covenant and grant to and with the said JOHN HENSLEY now is and standeth lawfully seized of and the said one hundred acres of Land and premises with the appurtenances of a good sure perfect absolute & indefesible estate in fee simple, and now hath good right full power and lawfull and absolute authority to grant & convey the same according to the purport true intend & meaning of these presents and that it shall & may be Lawfull to and for the said JOHN HENSLEY his heirs and assigns from time to time

and at all times forever hereafter peaceably and Quietly to have hold occupy possess use and enjoy the said one hundred acres of Land above bounded & all & singular other the premises herein before mentioned and intended to be hereby granted with their and every of their appurtenances without any lawfull Lott Suit Trouble or Molestation of him the said BENJAMIN HENSLEY his heirs or assigns or any other person or persons whatsoever discharged of and from all Incumbrances or Evictions whatsoever the Quitrents henceforth to Grow due to our Sovereign Lord the King his heirs and Successors only excepted and foreprized and the said BENJAMIN HENSLEY for himself his heirs Exors. & Admrs. the aforesaid Granted premises with the appurtenances unto the said JOHN HENSLEY his heirs against him the said BENJAMIN HENSLEY and his heirs & all claiming or to claim right in by from or under him them or any of them or any other person or persons Whatsoever shall and will warrant and forever Defend by these presents. In Witness whereof the said BENJAMIN HENSLEY to these presents hath interchangeably set his hand seal this day and year first above written. Signed Sealed and Delivered
in the presence of BENJAMIN HENSLEE [seal]
A. J. SMITH, WM. OGILVIE

Memorandum that peaceable and quiet possession of the premises within mentioned was had and taken by the within named BENJAMIN HENSLEY and by him delivered to the within mentioned JOHN HENSLEY to hold according to the within written Indenture.
A. J. SMITH, WM. OGILVIE BENJAMIN HENSLEE

p. <u>Louisa County Deed Book A 13th February 1744</u>
127 At a Court held for Louisa County on Monday the 13th day of February 1743.
This Indenture was this day in open Court acknowledged by BENJAMIN HENSLEY to be his act & deed & by the Court ordered to be recorded.
Test THOS. PERKINS Pr. JAS. LITTLEPAGE, Clk.

-This Indenture made the XIII day of February in the year of our Lord Christ MDCCXLIII Between JOHN FOSTER of the parish of Fredericksville in the County of Louisa & ANN his wife of the one part and SHIRWOOD HARRIS of the parish & County aforesaid of the other part. Witnesseth that the said JOHN FOSTER for divers good cause him thereunto moving but more especially for and in consideration of the sum of fifteen pounds current money of Virginia to them or one of them at or before the sealing and delivery of these presents in hand well & truly paid the receipt whereof they do hereby acknowledge and thereof and for every part thereof do hereby acquit & discharge the said SHIRWOOD HARRIS his heirs Exors. and Admors. forever by these presents Have granted bargained sold released enfeoffed & confirmed unto the said SHIRWOOD HARRIS and his heirs forever All that tract lott or parcel of Land & plantation of the said JOHN FOSTER situate & lying on both sides of Cub Creek in the said Parish of Fredericksville & County of Louisa and bounded as followeth [to wit] Beginning at pointers in WILLIAM HARRIS's line runing thence on the said line north fifty degrees east one hundred & sixty five poles crossing Creek to the Quik line, thence south forty two degrees east ninety poles to a pine thence south thirty eight degrees west one hundred & eighty eight poles crossing the said Creek to pointers thence south forty four degrees & a half east fifty poles to pointers, thence south fifty five degrees west twenty four poles to Pointers, thence north twenty four degrees west one hundred & ninety poles to the beginning place containing by estimation one hundred and four acres be the same more or less which said tract lott or parcel of Land and plantation was purchased by the said JOHN FOSTER by an Indenture of Feoffment bearing date the XIVth day of February in the year of our Lord MDCCXLII of one LAWRENCE REDMAN acknowledged & recorded in the Court of the said County of Louisa and reference being thereunto had may more at Large appear and all houses buildings fences gardens orchards woods underwoods ways waters privledges advantages & appurtenances whatsoever to the said tract or parcel of Land being or in any wise appertaining & the Reversion and Reversions Remainder and Remainders Rents Issues & profits thereof and of every part and parcell thereof & all the estate right title use interest property claim & demand is hereafter of the said JOHN FOSTER & ANN his wife or other of them their or other of their heirs and assigns of in to the same or any part or parcell thereof To Have and To Hold the said tract lott or parcel of Land & plantation & all & singular the premises herein before mentioned or intended to be hereby granted bargained & sold with their & every of their appurtenances unto the said SHIRWOOD HARRIS his heirs and assigns to his only proper use and behoof of the said SHIRWOOD HARRIS his heirs and assigns forever And the said JOHN FOSTER & ANN his said wife for themselves their heirs Exrs. & Admrs. doth covenant promise Grant & agree to & with the said SHIRWOOD HARRIS his heirs and assigns by these presents in manner and form following that is to say that they the said JOHN FOSTER & ANN his said wife now is and stands Lawfully seized of a Good Sure perfect absolute indefeasible estate of inheritance in fee simple and hath good right full power & authority to sell and convey the same in Manner and form aforesaid

p. <u>Louisa County Deed Book A 13th February 1744</u>
128 and that the said SHIRWOOD HARRIS his heirs & assigns shall & may forever hereafter peaceably & quietly have hold occupy possess & enjoy the same premises without the Lott Suit Molestation hindrance or disturbances of them the said JOHN FOSTER & ANN his wife or either of them their or either of their heirs & assigns or of any other person or persons whatsoever having or Lawfully claiming any right or like therein or thereto & that free & clear or freely & clearly acquitted & discharged or and from all former & other estates Rights & titles & of & from all judgments Executors debts mortgages & other incumberances whatsoever claiming any Estate Right Title or Interest of in or unto the premises or any part or parcell thereof by from or under the said JOHN FOSTER his heirs or assigns or otherwise shall and will at tall times hereafter upon the reasonable request and at the costs & charges in the Law of the said SHIRWOOD HARRIS his heirs or assigns make do perform acknowledge Levy & exenited or Suffer or cause to be made done performed acknowledged Levyed & exenited all & every such further & other Lawful & reasonable act and acts thing and things device and devises assurance and assurances conveyance and conveyances in the Land whatsoever for the further better and more perfect assuring sure making & conveying the said Land & premises with the appurtenances unto the said

SHIRWOOD HARRIS his heirs and assigns forever as by the said SHIRWOOD HARRIS or his counsel learned in the Law shall be reasonable devised advised or required and the said JOHN FOSTER and ANN his wife & their heirs all and singular the premises with the appurtenances unto the said SHIRWOOD HARRIS his heirs and assigns shall will warrant & forever defend by these presents. In Witness whereof the parties to these presents have interchangeably set their hands & seals the day & year first above written.

Sealed & delivered in presence of JOHN FOSTER [sea]
JEREMIAH GLENN, CHARLES NICHOLLS ANN X [her mark] FOSTER [seal]

Received the day & year first within written of the within named SHIRWOOD HARRIS the sum of [blank] pounds current money of Virginia being the consideration money within mentioned.

At a Court held for Louisa County on Monday the 13th day of February 1743.
This Indenture was this day in open Court acknowledged by JOHN FOSTER & ANN his wife to be their act and deed [the said ANN being first privily examined as the Law directs] & declaring her consent thereto & thereupon was by the Court ordered to be recorded.

Test THOMAS PERKINS Pr. JAS. LITTLEPAGE, Clk.

-This Indenture made this thirteenth day of February in the year of our Lord Christ one thousand seven hundred and forty three Between WILLIAM OGILIVE of the County of Louisa of the one part and JAMES COLEMAN of Orange County of the other part. Witnesseth that the said WILLIAM OGILIVE for and in consideration of the sum of fifteen pounds current money to him in hand paid by the said JAMES COLEMAN at & before the ensealing and delivery of the presents the receipt whereof he doth hereby acknowledge and thereof and of every part and parcel thereof doth clearly acquit & discharge the said JAMES COLEMAN his Exrs. & Admrs. & every of them by these presents hath granted aliened released enfeoffed & confirmed and by these presents doth grant alien release enfeoffe and perpetually confirm unto the said JAMES COLEMAN & to his heirs & assigns forever All that two hundred acres of Land between the two ledges of Mountains

p. <u>Louisa County Deed Book A 13th February 1744</u>
129 in the aforesaid County of Louisa and is bounded as followeth, to wit, beginning at WILLIAM CRADOCK's corner several marked trees, runing thence along his line north forty six degrees west one hundred and sixty poles to HOLEEN McGEE's corner white oake runing thence on his line north fifty three degrees east one hundred & eighty poles to pointers of bushes, thence on a new line south forty three degrees east two hundred poles to a pine saplin & a Spanish oak and south sixty six west one hundred & eighty poles to the beginning, which said two hundred acres of land above bounded in the moiety of four hundreds of land granted by patent bearing date the [blank] day of [blank] '73 to [unreadable] THY DALTON and by him conveyed to the said WILLIAM OLGIVIE by deeds proved & recorded in Hanover County Court and all the estate Right title interest use property and claim of in or unto the premises and the Reversion and Reversions Remainder and Remainders yearly & other Rents and profits of the premises and of every part and

parcel thereof To Have and To Hold the said two hundred acres of Land above bounded and all and singular other the premises herein before Mentioned and intended to be hereby granted with their appurtenances unto the said JAMES COLEMAN & his heirs to the only use of the said JAMES COLEMAN and of his heirs and assigns forever and the said WILLIAM OGILVIE for himself his heirs Exors. & Admors. doth covenant and grant to and with the said JAMES COLEMAN his heirs and assigns by these presents that he the said WILLIAM OGILVIE now is and standeth Lawfully and Rightfully seised of and in the said two hundred acres of Land & premises with the appurtenances of a Good sure perfect absolute and indefeasible estate in fee simple and now hath Good Rightfull power and Lawfull & absolute authority to grant and convey the same according to the purport true intent & meaning of these presents and that it shall & may be Lawfull to and for the said JAMES COLEMAN his heirs and assigns from time to time and at all times forever hereafter peaceably and Quietly to have hold occupy possess use and enjoy the said two hundred acres of land above bounded & all & singular other the premises herein before mentioned & intended to be hereby granted with their & every of their appurtenances without any Lawfull Lot Suite Trouble or Interruption of him the said WILLIAM OGILVIE his heirs or assigns or any other person or persons whatsoever discharged of and from all Incumbrances or Evictions whatsoever the Quitrents from henceforth to Grow due to our Sovereign Lord the King his heirs and Successors only excepted and foreprized, And the said WILLIAM OGILVIE for himself his heirs Exors. and Admors. the aforesaid Granted premises with the appurtenances unto the said JAMES COLEMAN & his heirs against him the said WILLIAM OGILVIE and his heirs and assigns claiming or to claim right in by from or under him them or any of them or any other person or person whatsoever shall and will warrant and forever defend by these presents. In Witness whereof the said WILLIAM OGILIVIE to these presents interchangeably set his hand & affixed his seal the day & year first above written.

Signed Sealed & delivered in presence of

THOMAS SMITH, JOSEPH PHILLIPS WILLIAM OGILVIE [seal]

Memorandum that peaceable and quiet possession of the premises within mentioned was had & taken by the within named WILLIAM OGILVIE and by him delivered to the within named JAMES COLEMAN to be by him held according to the within Indenture.
At a Court held for Louisa County on Monday the 13th day of February 1743.

p. Louisa County Deed Book A 13th February 1744

130 This Indenture was this day in open Court acknowledged by WILLIAM OGILVIE to be his act & deed & by the Court Ordered to be recorded.

Test THOMAS PERKINS Pr. JAMES LITTLEPAGE, Clk.

-This Indenture made the thirteenth day of February in the year of our Lord Christ one thousand seven hundred and forty three Between BURGIS HARRALSON of the parish of St. Paul in the County of Hanover of the one part and JOHN WALTON of the parish of St. Martin in the County aforesaid of the other part. In Witness that the said BURGIS HARRALSON for and in consideration of the sum of twenty pounds current money of Virginia to him in hand paid by the said JOHN WALTON at and before the ensealing and delivery of these presents the receipt whereof the said BURGIS HARRALSON doth hereby acknowledge and thereof and of every part and parcell thereof doth freely acquit Exonerate & discharged the said JOHN WALTON his heirs Exors. & Admors. by these presents hath given granted bargained sold aliened enfeoffed and confirmed and by these presents for him and his heirs doth fully clearly and absolutely give grant bargain sell alien enfeoffe and confirm unto the said JOHN WALTON and his heirs All that tract or parcell of land lying and being in the County of Louisa containing by estimation four hundred acres be the same more or less and bounded as followeth to wit beginning at WILLIAM CHAMBERS and MATTHEW SIMS corner pine runing thence along CHAMBERS line north twenty eight degrees west one hundred & twenty six poles to several pines thence north forty degrees west one hundred & twenty poles to a black oak saplin by a great pine in the said CHAMBER's line thence north eighteen degrees west forty three poles to a pine in POUNCY ANDERSON's line, thence along the said line north forty six degrees west thirty five poles to a pine, thence north thirty nine degrees west eighty one poles to ROBERT HOOD's corner hickory by a branch in ANDERSON's line thence along HOOD's line eighty nine degrees west one hundred & thirty poles to several pines in the said Line, thence south thirty three degrees east two hundred and eighty three poles to two pines and a Spanish oak in WILLIAM CHAMBERLAYN's line, thence along his line south eighty degrees west one hundred and eighteen poles to a juniper stump, thence south nine degrees east fifty two poles to MATTHEW SIM's line south eighty four degrees west eighty one poles to the beginning which said Land was Granted to PETER HARRALSON by patent bearing date the twelfth day of September one thousand seven hundred and thirty three with all woods underwoods ways waters and water courses meadows feedings pastures easements commodities hereditaments & appurtenances to the said premises belonging or in any wise appertaining and the Reversion and Reversions Remainder and Remainders and all the Estate Right Title Interest proper claim and demand whatsoever of him the said BURGIS HARRALSON of and in the premises or any part thereof with the appurtenances To Have and To Hold the said tract or parcel of Land and all and singular the premises with their and every of their appurtenances unto the said JOHN WALTON & his heirs to the only proper use and behoof of him the said JOHN WALTON his heirs and assigns forever and the said BURGIS HARRALSON the Lands and premises before mentioned with the appurtenances unto the said JOHN WALTON against him the said BURGIS HARRALSON his heirs &c. and all and every other person or persons claiming or to claim by from or under him them or any of them shall and will warrant and forever defend by these presents. In Witness whereof the said BURGIS HARRALSON

p. <u>Louisa County Deed Book A 13th February 1744</u>

131 to these presents his hand & seal hath set the day and year above written.

Sealed and delivered in the presence of

JOHN LONGAN, WM. DARWIN BURGIS HARRALSON [seal]

Memorandum that on the thirteenth day of February 1743/4 Livery & Seisin of the Land and premises within mentioned was given to the within named JOHN WALTON.

Test JOHN LONGAN, WM. DARWIN BURGIS HARRALSON [seal]
At a Court held for Louisa County on Monday the 13th day of February 1743.
This Indenture was this day in open Court acknowledged by BURGIS HARRALSON to be his act and deed & by the Court ordered to be recorded.
Teste THOMAS PERKINS Pr. JAMES LITTLEPAGE, Clk.

-This Indenture made this fourteenth day of November in the seventeenth year of the Reign of our Sovereign Lord George the second by the Grace of God of Great Britain France and Ireland King Defender of the Faith &c. and in the year of our Lord Christ one thousand seven hundred forty and three Between JOHN BLALOCK Senior of the parish of St. Martin in the County of Louisa planter of the one part and JOHN ANDERSON of the parish of St. Paul in the county of Hanover planter of the other part. Witnesseth that the said JOHN BLALOCK for and in consideration of the sum of fifty pounds current money of Virginia in hand paid or ensured to be paid at or before the ensealing & delivery of these presents these presents whereof to the said JOHN BLALOCK doth hereby confess and acknowledge & thereof & for every part and parcell thereof doth clearly acquit & discharge the said JOHN ANDERSON his heirs Exors. & Admors. forever by these presents he the said JOHN BLALOCK hath given granted bargained & sold aliened enfeoffed & confirmed and by these presents doth fully freely & absolutely give grant bargain sell alien enfeoff and confirm unto the said JOHN ANDERSON & to his heirs & assigns forever all that the said JOHN BLALOCK his tract or parcell of Land containing two hundred and six acres be the same more or less situate lying and being on both sides HARRIS's fork of Cub Creek in the parish of St. Martin in the County of Louisa aforesaid being part of four hundred acres granted to WILLIAM HARRIS by patent by him conveyed to the said JOHN BLALOCK by deed and bounded thus Vizt. Beginning at several marked pines in the Road runing thence North forty east sixty four to a pine, thence north twenty five degrees east forty one pole to several marked trees thence south fifty four degrees thirty minutes east at twenty four poles HARRIS's fork of Cub Creek in all two hundred and fifty three poles to a white oak, thence south forty nine & an half west one hundred & fifty one poles to a white oak in JOHN BLALOCK, Junior his line & along the same north fifty two west one hundred and seventy eight poles to his corner hickory by the aforesaid Creek, thence up the same by the meanders making in a strait line hereby two poles to the bridge, thence up the road to the first station with the Rights members & appurtenances thereof & all houses edifices buildings fences orchards gardens Lands meadows commons pastures feedings trees woods underwoods water and water courses easements commodities advantages hereditaments & appurtenances whatsoever to the said tract or parcel of two hundred & six acres of Land belonging or in any wise claiming and also the Reversion or Reversions Remainder and Remainders Rents & Services of all & singular the said premises above mentioned & of every part & parcell thereof with the appurtenances and also all the estate right title interest claim & demand whatsoever as well in Equity as in Law of him the said JOHN BLALOCK, Senior of in & to all & singular the said premises above mentioned

p. Louisa County Deed Book A 13th February 1744
132 and of in and to every part and parcell thereof with the appurtenances To Have and To Hold the said two hundred & six acres of Land & all & singular the premises above mentioned & part & parcell thereof with the appurtenances unto the said JOHN ANDERSON his heirs & assigns to the only proper use & behoof of the said JOHN ANDERSON his heirs and assigns forever And the said JOHN BLALOCK, Senior for himself his heirs & assigns doth covenant & grant to and with the said JOHN ANDERSON his heirs & assigns that to the said JOHN ANDERSON his heirs & assigns shall and may at all times for ever hereafter peaceably and quietly have hold occupy possess & enjoy all & singular the said Land and premises above mentioned to be hereby granted & sold with the appurtenances without the Lot hindrances molestation interruption & denial of him the said JOHN BLALOCK, Senior his heirs or assigns & of all & every other person or persons whatsoever and that freed & discharged or other use well & sufficiently saved & kept harmless & indemnified of & from all former & other bargains sales gifts grants Leases Mortgages Joynters dowers Wills Intails Fines Seizures bonds annuities writings obligatory Recognizances Extents Judgments and Exenitions Tents & arrearages of Rents and of and from all other charges estates Rights Titles Troubles & incumbrances whatsoever and further that he the said JOHN BLALOCK, Senior and his heirs & all & every other person or persons & his & their heirs anything having or claiming in the said premises above mentioned or any part thereof by from or under him shall & will from time to time & at all times hereafter upon the Reasonable Request & at the costs & charges of the said JOHN ANDERSON his heirs & assigns made do & exenite or cause or proved to be made done & opened all & every such farther & other Lawfull & reasonable act & acts thing & things device & devices conveyance and conveyances of all & singular the said premises as above mentioned with the appurtenances unto the said JOHN ANDERSON his heirs & assigns to the only proper use & behoof of the said JOHN ANDERSON his heirs & assigns forever as by the said JOHN ANDERSON his heirs or assigns or his or their Councele Learned in the Law shall be reasonably devised or advised or required And the said JOHN BLALOCK, Senior for himself & his heirs the said Lands & premises hereby bargained & sold with the appurtenances & every part thereof against him and his heirs & against all & every other person & persons whatsoever to the said JOHN ANDERSON his heirs & assigns shall & will warrant & forever defend by these presents. In Witness whereof the parties to these presents their hands & seals interchangeable set have set and affixed & delivered the day & year first above written.

Signed Sealed & delivered in the presence of
BARTTELOT ANDERSON, JOHN LONGAN, JOHN PRYOR JOHN BLALOCK [seal]
CHARLES SMITH

Memorandum that on the day & year first within written full possession was had & taken of the said Land & premises within granted by the within named JOHN BLALOCK, Senior & by him delivered over unto the within named JOHN ANDERSON to hold for him & his heirs forever according to the contents of the within written Indenture.

In presence of BARTTELOT ANDERSON
JOHN LONGAN, JOHN PRYOR, CHARLES SMITH JOHN BLALOCK

Received the fourteenth day of November MDCCXLIII of Mr. JOHN ANDERSON the full sum of fifty pounds current money being the consideration money for the Land & premises within granted & sold ordered the same by JOHN BLALOCK [seal]

p. Louisa County Deed Book A 13th February 1744
133 Witness BARTTELOT ANDERSON, JOHN LONGAN, JOHN PRYOR, CHARLES SMITH

At a Court held for Louisa County on Monday the 13th day of February 1743. This Indenture was this day in open Court proved to be the act & deed of JOHN BLALOCK, Senior by the oaths of JOHN LONGAN, JOHN PRYOR & CHARLES SMITH witnesses thereto & by the Court ordered to be recorded. JAMES LITTLEPAGE, Clk.

-This Indenture made the forth day of February in the year of our Lord one thousand seven hundred forty three Between ANDREW HUNTER of the parish of Saint Martin in the County of Louisa planter of the one part, and GEORGE WEBB of the parish of Saint Peter in the County of New Kent, Gentleman of the other part. Witnesseth that the said ANDREW HUNTER in consideration of the sum of sixteen pounds current money to him in hand paid before sealing & delivery of these presents the receipt whereof he doth hereby acknowledge hath granted bargained sold aliened enfeoffed & confirmed and by these presents doth grant bargain sell alien enfeoff & confirm unto the said GEORGE WEBB & his heirs and against all that tract or parcel of land situate lying and being in the parish of Fredericksville in the aforesaid County of Louisa and containing by estimation two hundred acres bounded as follows Vizt. beginning at a white oak corner tree between ROBERT DEPRIEST and the said GEORGE WEBB thence along DEPRIEST's line to several marked saplins, thence along ISAAC JOHNSON's Line to a corner pine near the main Road, thence cross the road to another corner Line in ROGER THOMPSON's line, thence to a corner red oak in the aforesaid WEBB's line, and thence along the Line aforesaid mentioned to the beginning the same being the remaining moiety and residue of a greater tract or four hundred acres granted to the said ANDREW HUNTER by patent bearing date at Williamsburg the fourth day of March MDCCXXV as by the said patent remaining of record lately by the said ANDREW HUNTER sold and conveyed to ISAAC JOHNSON and all buildings ways waters woods profits and emoluments whatsoever to the said first mentioned tract of two hundred acres belonging or appertaining and the Reversion & reversions Remainder and Remainders thereof and of every part and parcel thereof and all right title and interest whatsoever of him the said ANDREW HUNTER in and to the said bargained premises and every part and parcel thereof To Have and To Hold the said tract of land & all & singular the premises with the appurtenances unto the said GEORGE WEBB his heirs & assigns to the only proper use & behoof of him the said GEORGE WEBB his heirs and assigns forever, and the said ANDREW HUNTER his heirs and assigns the said tract of land & all & singular the premises with their appurtenances to the said GEORGE WEBB his heirs & assigns shall & will warrant and forever defend by these presents against all persons whatsoever having or lawfully claiming right or title in or to the same or any part thereof and the said ANDREW HUNTER for himself his heirs and Admors. doth covenant & grant to and with the said GEORGE WEBB his heirs &

assigns that he the said ANDREW now is and stands seised of an indefeasible estate of inheritance in fee simple in the said Lands & premises and hath full power and absolute authority to sell & convey the same in manner aforesaid, and that the said GEORGE WEBB his heirs and assigns shall and may forever hereafter peaceably & quietly have hold possess and enjoy all singular the premises & appurtenances without suit or molestation of any person or persons having or lawfully claiming right or title in or to the same or any part thereof and that the said tract of land and premises with the appurtenances shall be and for ever remain unto the said GEORGE WEBB his heirs & assigns freed and discharged of all other Rights titles dowers judgments arrears of Quitrents & all other Incumbrances whatsoever. In Witness whereof the said parties to these presents interchangeably have set sealed and delivered in presence of us

ROGER THOMPSON, DAVID PARKER, ANDREW HUNTER [seal]
WILLIAM X [his mark] CORMICK, DAVID X [his mark] CORMICK

p. <u>Louisa County Deed Book A 12th March 1744</u>
134 Received of GEORGE WEBB sixteen pounds the full consideration money in this deed within mentioned. Witness

ROGER THOMPSON, DAVID PARKER, ANDREW HUNTER [seal]
WILLIAM X [his mark] CORMICK, DAVID X [his mark] CORMICK

Memorandum that on this forth day of February MDCCXLIII Livery of Seisin of the Land and premises in this deed within granted and sold was made by the said ANDREW HUNTER unto the said GEORGE WEBB his heirs & assigns forever and being to the form and effort of the within Indenture. Executed before us

ROGER THOMPSON, DAVID PARKER ANDREW HUNTER [seal]

At a Court held for Louisa County on Monday the 12th day of March 1743.
This Indenture & Memorandum of livery of seisin & receipt endorsed were this day in open Court acknowledged by ANDREW HUNTER & by the Court ordered to be recorded.

Test THOMAS PERKINS Pre. JAMES LITTLEPAGE, Clk.

-This Indenture made this twelfth day of March in the year of our Lord Christ one thousand seven hundred and forty [blank] Between WILLIAM BIGGERS of Louisa County of the one part and STEPHEN ENGLISH of the same County of the other part. Witnesseth that the said WILLIAM BIGGERS for and in consideration of the sum of five pounds current money of Virginia to him in hand paid by the said STEPHEN ENGLISH before the ensealing and delivery of these presents the receipt whereof he doth hereby acknowledge & thereof & of every part and parcel of the same doth hereby acquit & discharge the said STEPHEN ENGLISH his Executors & Administrators and every of the by these presents hath granted aliened released enfeoffed & confirmed and by these presents for the consideration above set down doth grant alien release and perpetually confirm unto the said STEPHEN ENGLISH and to his heirs and assigns forever all that fifty acres of land [being part of four hundred acres] which is made over to the said WILLIAM BIGGERS by WILLIAM CARR on the west side of the Little Mountains in the aforesaid County and is bounded as followeth [to wit]

Beginning at BENJAMIN HENSLEY corner pine runing thence on his Line North forty four degrees east eighty poles to pointer's in the said Line thence south eighty three east one hundred & twenty two poles to pointers south forty six poles to pointers and north eighty eight degrees west one hundred seventy six poles to the first tree and all the estate Right Title interest use property claim & demand whatsoever to him the said WILLIAM BIGGERS his heirs or assigns of in or unto the premises and the Reversion & Reversions Remainder and Remainders yearly & other Rents profits of the premises & of every part and parcell thereof To Have and To Hold the said fifty acres of Land above bounded and all and singular other the premises herein before mentioned and intended to be hereby granted with all and every of their appurtenances unto the said STEPHEN ENGLISH and of his heirs & assigns forever And the said WILLIAM BIGGERS for himself his heirs Exors. & Admors. doth covenant & grant to and with the said STEPHEN ENGLISH his heirs & assigns by these presents that he the said WILLIAM BIGGERS now is & standeth Lawfully & Rightfully seised of and in the said fifty acres of Land & premises with the appurtenances of a Good sure perfect absolute and indefeasible estate in fee simple and now hath good rightfull power and lawfull and absolute authority to grant and convey the same according to the purport true intent & meaning of these presents and that it shall & may be Lawfull to and for the said STEPHEN ENGLISH his heirs & assigns from him to time to time and at all times forever hereafter peaceably and quietly to have hold occupy possess use and enjoy the said fifty acres of Land above bounded and

p. <u>Louisa County Deed Book A 12th March 1744</u>

135 premises with their & every of their appurtenances without any Lawfull Lot Suit Trouble or hindrance or Molestation of him the said WILLIAM BIGGERS his heirs or assigns or any other person or persons whatsoever discharged of and from all Incumbrances or Evictions whatsoever the quitrents from henceforth to grow due to our sovereign Lord the King only excepted and foreprized, and the said WILLIAM BIGGERS for himself his heirs Exors. & Admors. the aforesaid granted premises with their appurtenances unto the said STEPHEN ENGLISH his heirs against him the said WILLIAM BIGGERS and his heirs and all claiming or to claim Right in by form or under him them or any of them of any other person or persons whatsoever shall & will warrant and forever defend by these presents. In Witness whereof the said WILLIAM BIGGERS to these presents hath interchangeably set his hand and affixed his seal the day and year first above written.

In the presence of us

JOHN STARKE, BENJAMIN HENSLEE, JOHN McCARTEY WILLIAM BIGGERS [seal]

Memorandum that peaceable and quiet possession of the premises within mentioned was had and taken by the within named WILLIAM BIGGERS and by him delivered to the within named STEPHEN ENGLISH to be by him held according to the within written Indenture.

JOHN STARKE, BENJAMIN HENSLEE, JOHN McCARTEY WILLIAM BIGGERS [seal]

At a Court held for Louisa County on Monday the 12th day of March 1743.

This Indenture was this day in open Court acknowledged by WILLIAM BIGGERS also MARTHA the wife of the said WILLIAM [being first privily examined] relinquished all her right & title of dower of in and unto the Lands & appurtenances therein mentioned and ordered to be recorded. Test THOMAS PERKINS Pre. JAMES LITTLEPAGE, Clk.

-This Indenture made this twelfth day of March in the years of our Lord Christ one thousand seven hundred and forty three Between WILLIAM BIGGERS of Louisa County and SAMUEL BROCKMAN of Orange County of the other part. Witnesseth that the said WILLIAM BIGGERS for and in consideration of the sum of twenty five pounds current money of Virginia to him in hand paid by the said SAMUEL BROCKMAN and before the ensealing and delivery of these presents the receipt whereof he doth hereby acknowledge and thereof and of every part & parcell of the same doth clearly acquit & discharge the said SAMUEL BROCKMAN his Exors. & Admors. and or any of them by these presents hath granted aliened released enfeoffed and confirmed and by these presents doth grant alien release enfeoffed & perpetually confirm to the said SAMUEL BROCKMAN and to his heirs & assigns forever all that three hundred & fifty acres of Land on the west side of the Little Mountains in the aforesaid County of Louisa [being part of four hundred acres of Land conveyed by WILLIAM CARR unto the said WILLIAM BIGGERS by deed recorded in Hanover County Court and is bounded as followeth [to wit] Beginning at STEPHEN ENGLISH's corner pointers in BENJAMIN HENSLEE's line runing thence along the same north forty four degrees east two hundred fifty eight poles to his corner red oak stump and a white oak near a branch thence south fifty three degrees west one hundred ninety five poles to WILLIAM MEAD's corner white oak, thence on his Line south seven degrees west one hundred sixty nine poles to several saplins thence north eighty eight degrees west two hundred & ten poles to STEPHEN ENGLISH's corner pointer's thence on his lines north forty six poles to pointer's & north eighty eight degrees west one hundred & seventy six poles to the first station And all the estate Right Title interest use property & claim of him the said WILLIAM BIGGERS his heirs & assigns of in or unto the premises and the Reversion and Reversions Remainder & Remainders yearly & other Rents & profits of the premises & of every part and parcel thereof To Have and To Hold the said three hundred and fifty acres of Land above bounded with all singular other the premises herein before mentioned and intended to be hereby granted with their & every of their appurtenances to the said SAMUEL BROCKMAN and his heirs to the only use and behoof of him the said SAMUEL BROCKMAN & of his heirs & assigns forever And the said WILLIAM BIGGERS for himself

p. <u>Louisa County Deed Book A 12th March 1744</u>

136 his heirs Exors. and Admors. doth covenant grant to and with the said SAMUEL BROCKMAN his heirs & assigns by these presents, that he the said WILLIAM BIGGERS now is and standeth lawfully & rightfully seised of and in the said three hundred & fifty acres of Land and premises with the appurtenances of a good sure perfect absolute and indefeasible estate in fee simple and now hath good rightfull power and Lawfull and absolute authority to grant and convey the same according to the purport true intent & meaning of these presents and that it shall & may be Lawfull to & for the said SAMUEL BROCKMAN his heirs & assigns forever hereafter peaceably and Quietly to have hold occupy

possess use and enjoy the said three hundred & fifty acres of Land & premises with their appurtenances without the lawfull Lot suite Trouble hindrance or Molestation of him the said WILLIAM BIGGERS his heirs or assigns or any other person or persons whatsoever discharged of and from all Incumbrances or Evictions whatsoever the Quitrents from hereafter to Grow due to our Sovereign Lord the King only excepted and foreprized And the said WILLIAM BIGGERS for himself his heirs Exors. Admors. the aforesaid granted premises with the appurtenances unto the said SAMUEL BROCKMAN and his heirs against him the said WILLIAM BIGGERS & his heirs & all claiming or to claim Right in by from or under him them or any of them or any other person or persons whatsoever shall and will warrant and forever defend by these presents. In Witness whereof the said WILLIAM BIGGERS to these presents hath interchangeably set his hand and affixed his seal the day & year first above written.

Signed Sealed and delivered in the presence of
JOHN STARKE, BENJAMIN HENSLEE, JOHN McCARTEY WILLIAM BIGGER, SEN. [seal]
Memorandum that peaceable and Quiet possession of the premises within mentioned was had and taken by the within named WILLIAM BIGGERS and by him delivered to the within named SAMUEL BROCKMAN to be by him held according to the within mentioned Indenture.
JOHN STARKE, BENJAMIN HENSLEE, JOHN McCARTEY WILLIAM BIGGER, SEN. [seal]
At a Court held for Louisa County on Monday the XIIth day of March 1743.
This Indenture was this day in open Court acknowledged by WILLIAM BIGGER, also MARTHA the wife of the said WILLIAM [being first privily examined] relinquished all here Right & Title of Dower of in and unto the Lands & appurtenances therein mentioned.
Teste THOMAS PERKINS Pr. JAMES LITTLEPAGE, Clk.

-This Indenture made this twelfth day of March in the year of our Lord Christ one thousand seven hundred and forty three Between JOHN DAVIS of the parish of Fredericksville in the County of Louisa of the one part and ROBERT DAVIS of the aforesaid parish & County of the other part. Witnesseth that the said JOHN DAVIS for and in consideration of the sum of eight pounds current money of Virginia to him in hand paid by the said ROBERT DAVIS the Receipt whereof he doth hereby acknowledge and thereof and of every part and parcell of the same doth clearly acquit and discharge the said ROBERT DAVIS his Exors. & Admors. and every of them by these presents hath granted aliened released enfeoffed & confirmed and by these presents for the consideration above set down doth grant alien release enfeoff and perpetually confirm unto the said ROBERT DAVIS & his heirs & assigns for ever all that the said JOHN DAVIS his parcell or tract of Land containing one hundred and forty acres Lying on the branches of CHAMBERLAYNES and Poor Creek in the aforesaid parish & County and is bounded as followeth [to wit] Beginning at ROBERT NETHERLAND's corner two pines & a white oake runing thence on his line south sixty four degrees thirty minutes west one hundred & seventy his poles to JOHN RAGLAND corner several marked trees thence

p. Louisa County Deed Book A 12th March1744

137 on RAGLAND's lines south fifty five degrees east ninety poles to a red oak saplin and north fifty five east two hundred and sixty poles to RAGLAND's corner stake, thence north fifty degrees west one hundred and twenty poles to a pine, and south forty four degrees west one hundred & seventy poles to a pine by NETHERLAND line, thence along the same south forty nine degrees west forty poles to the beginning which said one hundred forty acres of Land is part of sixteen hundred and forty five acres granted to JOHN SMOTHING by patent bearing date the fifty day of June 1736 and by him twelve hundred and five acres of the same was made over unto the said JOHN DAVIS by Deeds acknowledged in Hanover County Court and all the estate Rights Title interest use property claim and demand whatsoever of the said JOHN DAVIS his heirs and assigns of in or unto the premises and the Reversion and Reversions Remainder and Remainders yearly and other Rents & profits of the premises and of every part and parcell thereof To Have and To Hold the said one hundred & forty acres of Land above bounded & all & singular other the premises herein before mentioned and intended to be hereby granted with their & every of their appurtenances unto the said ROBERT DAVIS & his heirs to the only use of the said ROBERT DAVIS and of his heirs and assigns forever And the said JOHN DAVIS for himself his heirs Exors. & Admors. doth covenant & grant to and with the said ROBERT DAVIS his heirs and assigns by these presents that he the said JOHN DAVIS now is and standeth Lawfully and Rightfully seised of & in the said one hundred & forty acres of Land above bounded & premises with their and every appurtenance of a good sure perfect and absolute and indefeasible estate in fee simple and now hath good Rightfull power and Lawfull and absolute authority to Grant and convey the same and according to the purport true intent & meaning of these presents and that it shall and may be Lawfull to and for the said ROBERT DAVIS his heirs and assigns for ever hereafter peaceably and Quietly to have hold occupy possess use and enjoy the said one hundred & forty acres of land above bounded and premises with their appurtenances without any Lawfull Lott Suite hindrance trouble or molestation of him the said JOHN DAVIS his heirs or assigns or any other person or persons whatsoever discharged from all incumbrances or Evictions whatsoever the Quitrents from henceforth to Grow due unto our Sovereign Lord the King his heirs and Successors only excepted and foreprized And the said JOHN DAVIS for himself his heirs Exors. & Admors. the aforesaid Granted premises with their appurtenances unto the said ROBERT DAVIS & his heirs against him the said JOHN DAVIS & his heirs and all claiming or to claim Right in by from or under him them or any of them or any of them or any other person or person whereof the said JOHN DAVIS to these presents hath interchangeably set his hands and affixed his seal the day and year first above written.

Signed Sealed and delivered in the presence of us

JOHN VENABLES, WM. SMITHSON JOHN DAVIS [seal]

Memorandum that peaceable and quiet possession of the premises within mentioned and taken by the within named JOHN DAVIS and by him delivered to the within named ROBERT DAVIS be by him held according to the within written Indenture. JOHN DAVIS

At a Court held for Louisa County on Monday the XIIth day of March 1743.

This Indenture was this day in open Court acknowledged by JOHN DAVIS, also SUSANNA the wife of the said JOHN [being first privily examined] relinquished all her Right & Title of dower unto the Lands & appurtenances therein mentioned and ordered to be recorded.

Teste THOMAS PERKINS Pre. JAMES LITTLEPAGE, Clk.

-This Indenture made this tenth day of April in the year of our Lord Christ one thousand seven hundred and fourty four Between PETER GARLAND, JUN. of Hanover County of the one part and ROBERT GARLAND of Louisa County of the other part. Witnesseth that the said JOHN GARLAND for and in consideration of the sum of fourty pounds current money of Virginia to him in hand paid by the said ROBERT GARLAND at and before the ensealing and Delivery of these presents the receipt unto the said PETER GARLAND doth hereby acknowledge Have granted bargained sold aliened released

p. <u>Louisa County Deed Book A 10th April 1744</u>

138 and confirmed & by the presents doth grant bargain sell alien release and confirm unto the said ROBERT GARLAND all that tract or parcell of Land situate lying and being in Louisa County on the Little River and Horse Pen Swamp containing one hundred acres more or less and bounded as followeth [to wit] beginning at the Mouth of the said Horse Pen Swamp runing up the same the several courses making in a strate line one hundred & thirty poles to a corner white oake thence south fourty four degrees east one hundred & eighteen poles to two red oaks thence south forty eight degrees west one hundred and eighteen poles to the Little River thence up the same the several courses to the beginning place with all horses Edifices Gardens Orchards woods underwoods pastures feedings & profits to the said Land belonging or in any wise appertaining and the Reversion & Reversions Remainder & Remainders thereof, and all the Right title interest claim & demand of him the said PETER GARLAND in or to the said Land & premises and every part To Have and To Hold the said tract or parcel of Land containing one hundred acres aforesaid and all and singular other the premises with their & every of their appurtenances unto the said ROBERT GARLAND his heirs and assigns for ever to the only proper use and behoof of him the said ROBERT GARLAND his heirs and assigns forever, And the said PETER GARLAND for himself his heirs Exors. & Admrs. and assigns in manner following that the said ROBERT GARLAND his heirs and assigns shall and may from time to time and at all times hereafter Quietly and peaceably have hold possess and enjoy the aforesaid Land & premises and every part thereof with the appurtenances without any Lawfull Lott Suit Trouble eviction or Molestation of him the said PETER GARLAND his heirs or assigns or of any other person or persons whatsoever claiming or to claim by from or under him them or any of them And that free and clear & freely & clearly acquited & discharged or by the said PETER GARLAND his heirs Exors. & Admrs. or some of them from time to time and at all times hereafter keep harmless and indemnified of and from all & all manner of former or other bargains sailes gifts grants intails dowers & Titles of Dowers & all other charges and Incumbrances whatsoever had under committed done or suffered by him the said PETER GARLAND the said Land and premises herein before bargained & sold with their & every of their

appurtenances unto the said ROBERT GARLAND his heirs & assigns shall and will warrant and forever defend by these presents. In Witness whereof he the said PETER GARLAND hath hereunto sett his hand and seal the year first above written. PETER GARLAND [seal]
Received of the within named ROBERT GARLAND fourty pounds current money it being the consideration money within mentioned I say received by me this Ninth day April one thousand seven hundred and fourty four. PETER GARLAND
At a Court held for Louisa County on Monday the Xth day of April 1744.
This Indenture and Receipt was this day in open Court acknowledged by PETER GARLAND to be his act & deed & by the Court admitted to record and is recorded.
Test THOMAS PERKINS Pr. JAMES LITTLEPAGE, Clk.

-To all to whom these presents shall come I DAVID MERIWETHER of the parish of Fredericksville County of Louisa send Greeting: Know ye that the said DAVID MERIWETHER for and in consideration of the Natural affection I bear to my well beloved son in law THOMAS BALLARD SMITH of the parish & County aforesaid also for divers other Good causes and considerations me at this presents moving hath given grant aliened enfeoffed and confirmed & by these presents doth fully clearly & absolutely give grant alien enfeoff & confirmed unto the said THOMAS BALLARD SMITH his heirs & assigns forever one certain tract or parcel of Land containing two hundred acres more or less lying & being in the parish & County aforesaid & bounded as followeth [to wit] beginning at a Spanish oak on the

p. <u>Louisa County Deed Book A 10th April 1744</u>

139 River Bank in MERIWETHER's line runing up the water courses snakeing in a straight line forty six poles to a maple & hiccory, thence into the woods North eighty three east eighty poles to a white oake, thence north forty five east one hundred & twenty poles to a pine thence North fifty four east one hundred & forty poles to a red oak & two hicory Grubs thence south forty east crossing Dirty Swamp one hundred & twenty poles to a corner pine, thence south fifty five west forty poles to Major. MERIWETHER's corner several marked trees, thence along his line south fifty five west one hundred & eighty poles crossing Dirty Swamp, thence to the beginning in all two hundred and forty poles with twelve acres was refered out of a former deed from me to JAMES GOODALL one acres & refered for myself to be laid out on a square including the old mill I also give to the said THOMAS BALLARD SMITH four Negroes namely BESS YORK WILL & SAM which said land & negroes I give to the said THOMAS BALLARD SMITH to be equally divided at the decease of the said THOMAS & ANNE his wife amongst the heirs of his body lawfully together by the said ANNE and me case there should be us such heir of the said SMITH & his wife should interinarry that then her issue shall enjoy this estate and for want of both such issue it is to go to FRANCIS MERIWETHER son of DAVID MERIWETHER which said land & negroes with there appurtenances shall give unto my aforesaid son in law THOMAS BALLARD SMITH with all woods underwoods low ground pastures ways waters & water courses profits & hereditaments and appurtenances whatsoever to the said parcel or tract of land belonging or in any wise appertaining & the Reversion Right Title interest property claim and demand

whatsoever of him the said DAVID MERIWETHER or to the premises or any part thereof with the appurtenances To Have and To Hold the said parcel or tract of land within mentioned and all & Singular other the premises herein before Granted or intended to be Granted with there and every of there appurtenances unto the said THOMAS BALLARD SMITH & his heirs as before mentioned And the said DAVID MERIWETHER for himself & his heirs the said Land and premises with the appurtenances unto the said THOMAS BALLARD SMITH & his heirs against him the said DAVID MERIWETHER heirs & assigns and all persons whatsoever Lawfully claiming or to claim by from or under them or any of them shall & will warrant and forever defend by these presents. In Witness whereof the said DAVID MERIWETHER hath set his hand & affixed his seal this ninth day of April 1744.

Signed Sealed & delivered in presence of us

JOSEPH COX, SAMUEL WADDY, THOMAS PERKINS DAVID MERIWETHER [seal]

At a Court for Louisa County on Monday the Xth day of April 1744.
This Indenture was this day proved in open Court to be the act & deed of the said DAVID MERIWETHER by the oaths of JOSEPH COX, SAMUEL WADDY & THOMAS PERKINS witnesses thereto & by the Court ordered to be recorded and is recorded.

Test JAMES LITTLEPAGE, Clk. Cur.

-Know all men by these presents that we JOSEPH BICKLEY & JOHN CARR are held and firmly bound unto our Sovereign Lord George the second &c. in the sum of thirty two thousand three hundred and ninety two pounds of Tobacco to be paid to our said Lord the King his heirs & successors to the which payment well & truly to be made We bind our Selves & every of us our & every of our heirs Exrs. & Admrs. jointly & severally firmly by these presents sealed with our seals dated this 9th day of April Anno dom. 1744.
The Condition of this obligation is such that if the above bounded JOSEPH BICKLEY shall duly collect the Levy laid and assessed on the Tithables persons within the aforesaid County of Louisa by the Court of the same County on the Xth day of October last and the same shall duly pay in

p. <u>Louisa County Deed Book A 10th April 1744</u>
140 such proportions & to such persons & for such uses & purposes as the same is directed by the said Court and as the Law in such case provides, then this obligation to be void or also to remain in full force & virtue.

Sealed and Delivered in presence of JO. BICKLEY [seal]
[blank] JOHN CARR [seal]

At a Court held for Louisa County on Monday the 10th day of April 1744.
This Indenture was this day in open Court acknowledged by JOSEPH BICKLEY & JOHN CARR, Gent. to be their act & deed & by the Court ordered to be recorded and is recorded.

Teste JAMES LITTLEPAGE, Clk.

-This Indenture made this XIV day of May in the year of our Lord MDCCXLIV by and between JOHN DAVIS of the one part and JAMES LASLEY of the other part. Witnesseth that the said DAVIS hath for and in the consideration of the sum of eleven pounds currant money of Virginia to him in hand allready paide and received hath given granted and by these presents doth absolutely alien the use of one hundred and twenty five acres of land be the same more or less according to the bounds thereof being part of a patten bearing date June the fifty MDCCXXVI and bounded as foloeth to with beginning at ROBERT NETHERLAND's corner two pines and white oaks thence along the said NETHERLAND;s line north forty nine degrees west all one hundred and twenty poles to Poors Creek thence down the said Creek by the water corce to FR. SMITHSON's corner white oak in the Creek thence along the said SMITHSON's line along the hill side to a corner in SMITHSON's line, thence runing in a Strate corce to the first station together with houses plantation and all other improvements upon the said CXXV acres of land to the same more or less according to the bounds thereof with all manner and all singular the members rights and heridatements and appurtenances whatsoever together with all and every deeds wrighting and evidence to the said Land or to any part or parcell thereof in any wise apertaining To Have and To Hold the said Land be the same more or less according to the bounds thereof and all and singular other the premises unto the said LASLEY his heirs and assigns forever and that in as firm ample maner to all intents and purposes as an estate in fee simple absolutely can be held or injoyed and shuch an estate in and for the premises the said DAVIS binds and oblidges himself his heirs and assigns by this Deede to warrant and forever against all manner of persons claiming under and pretence wright or Title whatsoever and allso that the said DAVIS he his heirs and assigns shall & unto shuch other Deeds and assurances for the better conveyance the premises by the true meaning of this Deede unto the said LASLEY his heirs and assigns and by him them or their council shall be required and to the performance true keeping and fullfilling of all and singular the premises artickels clauses and conditions of this deede the said DAVIS binds and oblidges himself his heirs Executors Administrators and assigns in the penal sum of CCL currant money of Virginia. In Witness within whereof the said DAVIS hath hereunto sett his hand and seale the day and year within written.

Signed Sealed and Delivered in the presence of us JOHN DAVIS [seal]
BENJA. HENSON, FR. SMITHSON

Memorandum that upon the XIV day of May in the year of our Lord MDCCXLIV ful and peaceable possession and seizure was given and Delivered by the within named JOHN DAVIS of the within mentioned CXXV acres of Land with the appurtenances unto the within named LASHLEY for and unto his use his heirs and assigns forever according to the true purport of this present Indenture. BENJA HENSON, FR. SMITHSON JOHN DAVIS

p. <u>Louisa County Deed Book A 14th May 1744</u>
141 At a Court held for Louisa County on Monday the XIV day of May 1744.

This Indenture was this day in open Court acknowledged by JOHN DAVIS to be his act and deed also SUSANNA the wife of the said JOHN [being first privily examined as the Law directs] did in open Court Relinquish unto JAMES LASLEY the right of Dower which she hath in the land conveyed by this Indenture & by the Court ordered to be recorded and is recorded. Teste THOMAS PERKINS Pr. JAMES LITTLEPAGE, Clk.

-Know all men by these presents that we THOMAS GREEN & DANIEL WILLIAMS of the County of Louisa are held and firmly bound unto ROBERT LEWIS the first Justice in the Commission of the Board for the said county for and in behalf and to the sole use and behoof of the Justices of the County and their Successors in the sum of two hundred pounds to be paid to the said ROBERT LEWIS his Exors. Admrs. And assigns to which payment well and truly to be made we bind ourselves and every of us our and every of our heirs Exors. and Admrs. Jointly & severally firmly by these presents sealed with our seals and dated this 14th day of May 1744.
The Condition of this obligation is such that if the above named THOMAS GREEN his Exrs. and Admrs. Shall well & truly pay and deliver or cause to be paid and delivered unto NATHANIEL CHAMBERS Orphan of WARD CHAMBERS deceased all such estate or estates as now is or are or hereafter shall appear to be due to the said Orphan when and as soon as he shall attain the age or when thereto required by the Justices of the said County Court as also keep harmless the above named ROBERT LEWIS and the rest of the said Justices their and every of their heirs Exrs. and Admrs. From all Trouble & damages that shall or may arise about the said estate then the above obligation to be void otherwise to remain in full force.

THOMAS GREEN [seal] DANIEL WILLIAMS [seal]

At a court held for Louisa County on Monday the XIV day of May 1744.
This Indenture was this day in open Court acknowledged by THOMAS GREEN & DANIEL WILLIAMS to be their act & deed & ordered to be recorded and is recorded.

Teste THOMAS PERKINS Pr. JAMES LITTLEPAGE, Clk.

-Know all men by these presents that we WILLIAM SLEDD, CHARLES RICE & WILLIAM RICE of the County of Louisa are held and firmly bound unto ROBERT LEWIS the first Justice in the Commission of the peace for the said County for and in behalf and to the sole use and behoof of the Justices of the said County & their Successors in the sum of one hundred pounds current money to be paid to the said LEWIS his Exors. Admors. and assigns to which payment well & truly to be under we bind ourselves and every of us our and every of our heirs Exors. and Admrs. Jointly & severally and firmly by these presents sealed with our Seals and dated this XIV day of May 1744.
The Condition of this obligation is such that if the above bound WILLIAM SLEDD his heirs Exrs. and Admrs. Shall well and truly pay and deliver or cause to be paid and delivered unto JOHN SLEDD orphan of DODMAN SLEDD deceased all such estate or estates as now is or are or hereafter shall appear to be due the said Orphan when and as soon as he shall attain to Lawfull age or when thereto required by the Justices of the said County Court as also keep harmless the above named ROBERT LEWIS and the rest of the Justices their and every of their heirs Exrs. and Admrs. From all trouble and damages that shall or may arise about the said estate, then the above obligation to be void otherwise to remain in full force.

WM. SLEDD [seal] CHARLES RICE [seal] WILLIAM RICE [seal]

At a Court held for Louisa County on Monday the 14th day of May 1744.

p. <u>Louisa County Deed Book A 14th May 1744</u>
142 This bond was this day in open Court acknowledged by WILLIAM SLEDD,

CHARLES RICE & WM. RICE to be their act & deed & ordered to be recorded & is recorded.
Teste THOMAS PERKINS Pr. JAMES LITTLEPAGE, Clk.

-This Indenture made this fifth day of May in the year of our Lord Christ one thousand seven hundred & forty four Between WILLIAM HAGGARD and ELIZABETH his wife of the parish of Overwharton in the County of Prince William of the one part and ELIAS THOMASON of the parish of St. Martin's in the County of Louisa of the other part. Witnesseth that the said WILLIAM HAGGARD & ELIZABETH his wife for and in consideration of the sum of ten pounds current money of Virginia to him in hand paid by the said ELIAS THOMASON at and before the ensealing and delivery of these presents doth bargain and sell alien and make over and confirm unto the said ELIAS THOMASON and to his heirs and assigns forever a certain tract or parcell of land containing one hundred and fifty acres lying and being on the branches of Golden Mine Creek in the County of Louisa bounded as followeth Virzt. Beginning at a shruby white oak runing thence south fifty eight degrees west two hundred poles to pointers north eighteen degrees west sixty two poles to pointers in a stake &c. North twelve degrees east one hundred sixty poles to pointers thence north seventy five degrees east thirty five poles to three pines by a small branch & south forty five degrees east one hundred eighty four poles to the first station; which said one hundred & fifty acres of land above bounded is part of twelve hundred acres granted to RICHARD ESTES who sold this land to the said WILLIAM HAGGARD by deed dated the first day of October one thousand seven hundred and forty one together with all the estate right title or interest of him the said HAGGARD or his heirs or any person or persons whatsoever with all the appurtenances to be truly granted unto the said ELIAS THOMASON and his heirs to the only use and behoof of the said ELIAS THOMASON his heirs or assigns from time to time and at all times hereafter without the Least hinderance of him the said HAGGARD his wife or any other person or persons whatsoever and him and them safe and indemnified will keep and maintain of and from all incumberances only the Quitrents to grow due to our Sovereign Lord the King only excepted and foreprized In of him any of which he hath hereto sett their hands and affixed their seals the day and year above written, interlined before signed.

JAMES HAGGARD WILLIAM HAGGARD [seal]
MARGARET X [her mark] HAGGARD ELIZABETH X [her mark] HAGGARD [seal]

Memorandum that full and peaceable possession and seized was this day given and delivered by the within WILLIAM HAGGARD & ELIZABETH his wife to ELIAS THOMASON of the Land and premises within mentioned in presence of us whose names are subscribed in Witness whereof the said WILLIAM HAGGARD hath hereunto set his hand and seal the day and year within mentioned.

JAMES HAGGARD WILLIAM HAGGARD
MARGARET X [her mark] HAGGARD ELIZABETH X [her mark] HAGGARD

This day received of the within named ELIAS THOMASON the sum of ten pounds current money of Virginia being the consideration within mentioned. Witness my hand this fifth day of May one thousand seven hundred and forty five.

WILLIAM HAGGARD

At a Court held for Louisa County on Monday the XIth day of June 1744.
This Indenture & Memorandum of livery of seisin & receipt were this day in open court acknowledged by WILLIAM HAGGARD & ELIZABETH his wife to be their act & deed the said ELIZABETH being first privily examined as the Law directs & declaring her consent thereto & thereupon it was by the Court ordered to be recorded and

p. Louisa County Deed Book A 11th June 1744
143 is recorded. Teste THOMAS PERKINS Pr. JAMES LITTLEPAGE, Clk.

-This Indenture made this twenty first day of February in sixteenth year of the Reign of our Sovereign Lord George the second by the Grace of God of Great Britain France and Ireland King Defender of the faith and in the year of our Lord Christ one thousand seven hundred and forty three Between JOHN McQUERRY of Saint Martin's Parish in the County of Louisa of the one part and JAMES UNDERWOOD of the aforesaid Parish in the County of Hanover of the other part. Witnesseth that the said JOHN for and in consideration of the sum of eighty pounds current money of Virginia to him in hand paid by the said THOMAS at and before the ensealing and delivery of these presents the receipt whereof he the said JOHN doth hereby acknowledge and himself therewith to be fully contented satisfied and paid and thereof and of every part and parcell thereof doth acquit exonerate and discharge the said THOMAS his heirs Executors Administrators and assigns Hath given granted bargained sold aliened enfeoffed and conveyed and by these presents for himself his heirs Executors Administrators and every of them doth give grant bargain sell alien enfeoff convey release and confirm unto the said THOMAS UNDERWOOD and his heirs and assigns forever all that three hundred acres of Land and Plantation thereon lying and being in the aforesaid parish of St. Martin's in the County of Louisa and Hanover it being the Land and plantation whereon the said JOHN McQUERRY now liveth and part of four hundred acres of Land granted to the said JOHN by patent dated the twentieth day of February one thousand seven hundred and twenty three with all houses buildings gardens orchards woods underwoods ways waters Rivers water courses swamps meadows pastures yearly and other rents issues and profits benefits emoluments and advantages on the same being or to the same or any part thereof in any wise appertaining and the Reversion and Reversions remainder and remainders of the said three hundred acres of Land and premises be the same more or less To Have and To Hold the said above granted and sold land and premises with the appurtenances and every part and parcell thereof to the said THOMAS UNDERWOOD and his heirs and assigns forever And the said JOHN for himself his heirs Executors Administrators doth covenant grant bargain and agree to and with the said THOMAS his heirs Executors Administrators and assigns that it shall and May be Lawfull to and for the said THOMAS his heirs and assigns from time to time and at all times forever hereafter peaceably and quietly to have hold use occupy possess and enjoy all and singular the above granted and sold Land and premises with the appurtenances and every part and parcell thereof free and clear of any Lawful set suit hinderance or molestation of him the said JOHN his heirs Executors or Administrators or any other person claiming any right or title to the same or any part thereof by from or under him them or any of them And that he the said JOHN the said Land and premises with the appurtenances and every part and parcell thereof against him the said JOHN his heirs Executors Administrators and all claiming or pretending to claim any Right or title thereto or unto any part thereof by from or under him them or any of them unto the said THOMAS and to his heirs and assigns will forever warrant and defend by these presents. In Witness whereof the said parties to these presents their hands and seals have interchangeably sett the day and year first above written.

Signed Sealed and Delivered in the presence of us

DAVID HARRIS, GEORGE TOMSON JOHN X [his mark] McQUERRY [seal]

THOMAS FARMBROUGH

Memorandum that on the day and year within mentioned peaceable and quiet possession and seisin of the within mentioned Land and premises was had and taken by the within named JOHN McQUERRY and by him delivered unto the within named THOMAS UNDERWOOD according to the tenor of the act and deed In presence of us

DAVID HARRIS, GEORGE TOMSON JOHN X [his mark] McQUERRY [seal]

THOMAS FARMBROUGH

Received February 1743/4 of THOMAS UNDERWOOD Eighty pounds current money of Virginia it being the consideration money for the within granted and sold land and premises with the appurtenances I say received by me £100

Test DAVID HARRIS, GEORGE TOMSON, THOMAS FARMBROUGH

JOHN X [his mark] McQUERRY [seal]

p. <u>Louisa County Deed Book A 11th June 1744</u>

144 At a Court held for Louisa County on Monday the XIth day of June 1744.

This Indenture & Memorandum of livery of seisin & receipt for the consideration money endorsed were this day in open Court acknowledged by JOHN McQUERRY to be his act & deed & by the Court ordered to be recorded.

Teste THOMAS PERKINS Pr. JAMES LITTLEPAGE, Clk.

This day also ELIZABETH the wife of the said JOHN being first privily examined as the Law directs & declaring here consent thereto did in open Court relinquish unto THOMAS UNDERWOOD the Right of Dower which she hath in the Land conveyed by this Indenture & the same by the Court was admitted to record and is recorded.

Teste THOMAS PERKINS Pr. JAMES LITTLEPAGE, Clk.

This Louisa County Deed Book A 1742 - 1754 will continue in the next book which continues on June 11 1744 with the Indenture between Capt. Joseph Temple and Clevers Duke.

INDEX, LOUISA COUNTY, VA. 1742 TO 1744

INDEX, LOUISA COUNTY, VA. 1742 TO 1744

INDEX, LOUISA COUNTY, VA. 1742 TO 1744

INDEX, LOUISA COUNTY, VA. 1742 TO 1744

INDEX, LOUISA COUNTY, VA. 1742 TO 1744

www.ingramcontent.com/pod-product-compliance
Lightning Source LLC
LaVergne TN
LVHW061250100826
845148LV00008B/1077
* 9 7 8 1 6 8 0 3 4 3 9 8 4 *